FEB 2 1

A Light Has Dawned is a one-of-a-kind book that excels in every possible way. It surpasses any book of Christmas devotions that I have read. Variety is one of the most obvious virtues of the book. As the list of authors keeps accumulating, the angles of vision on Christmas likewise keep expanding. The effect is like turning a prism in the light. This is a "best of the best" book—the best evangelical authors giving us the best of their Christmas insights.

We do not ordinarily think of a book of devotions as a triumph of scholarship, but that is exactly what this book is, as the editor did the research required to find the selections that are offered to us. I found the book to be a page-turner, as I wondered who would be next on the playlist, and what aspect of Christmas would be the focus of meditation. I dare to predict that anyone who reads this book will be unable to envision any future Christmas without rereading it.

LELAND RYKEN
professor emeritus of English,
Wheaton College

A Light Has Dawned

Meditations on
Advent and Christmas

A Light Has Dawned

Meditations on Advent and Christmas

Best of *Christianity Today*

LEXHAM PRESS

A Light Has Dawned: Meditations on Advent and Christmas
Best of Christianity Today

Print ISBN 9781683594222
Digital ISBN 9781683594239
Library of Congress Control Number 2020941280

Lexham Editorial: Elliot Ritzema, Danielle Thevenaz
Cover Design: Joshua Hunt
Typesetting: Fanny Palacios, Abigail Stocker

Contents

✧

Introduction

Carolyn Arends

Perhaps, like me, you have a fondness for puns. If so, here are a few Advent gifts for you.

I know a guy who's addicted to brake fluid. He says he can stop anytime.

I'm reading a book on anti-gravity. I can't put it down.

Don't trust atoms. They make everything up.

I stayed up all night to see where the sun went. Then it dawned on me.

Here's the thing about that last one. It's been dawning on me (pun intended) that there is an important Advent invitation beating right at the heart of that otherwise-silly pun.

Imagine the first dawn after the birth of Jesus. Picture an exhausted Joseph, holding his adopted newborn in the aftermath of a very strange night, rubbing his bleary eyes and suddenly remembering the words of the prophet Isaiah:

> The people walking in darkness
>   have seen a great light;
> on those living in the land of deep darkness
>   a light has dawned. (Isaiah 9:2 NIV)

That first Christmas morning, was Joseph capable of beholding the great light right before his eyes? Could he grasp what was taking place? To whatever extent he reached an understanding, did it come to him in a flash, or did it take a while?

I'm willing to bet it took some time. Human eyes can only take in so much light at once. Our brains can only comprehend so much so fast. Our hearts need time to expand.

Counterintuitively, the more glorious something is, the longer it takes to dawn on us.

E very year, whether we're ready for it or not, we're offered a fresh chance to take in the blazing miracle of the incarnation—God becoming flesh, the Light of the World moving into the neighborhood (John 1:14 MES-SAGE). And yet, how many Christmases have we missed the glory entirely, captured by lesser lights, allowing ourselves to be spent (both literally and figuratively) attending to a thousand distractions?

Oh, how we need the season of Advent. On the Christian calendar, Advent always begins the fourth Sunday before Christmas. This means, depending on the year, Advent can begin as early as November 27 or as late as December 3, offering us a three-to-four week season of preparation and longing. When we observe Advent with intentionality, we give ourselves the chance to take in a bit more of the light each day: adjusting our eyes, cali-brating our hearts, preparing him room.

I t's no coincidence that this book of Advent and Christmas reflections is entitled *A Light Has Dawned*. The articles in these pages were all written for

Christianity Today over a sixty-year period. Certainly, the pieces vary to some extent in style and tone. But there is a remarkable cohesion around the invitation to attend to the light.

In the first piece in this collection, for example, Alice Slaikeau Lawhead is struck afresh by an astonishing line in the Christmas Eve liturgy: *In the morning you shall see the glory of the Lord.*

A few entries later, Katelyn Beaty reminds us that the incarnation can't be "sold, scheduled, or enjoyed in the way a glass of eggnog or a new gadget can," but rather "can only be beheld." Beaty also warns us that the light might not appear in the ways that we expect, even as she reassures us that Jesus "waits for our eyes to adjust to the dim light emanating from the manger." Her words, written in 2015, resonate with reflections offered by Donald J. Shelby twenty-five years earlier: "God 'came down the backstairs at Bethlehem,' wrote [George] Buttrick, 'lest he blind us by excess of light.' "

Mary Ellen Ashcroft, on the other hand, rounds out the picture by asking us to remember that we find Christ not only sleeping in the manger but also ruling on the throne. Here, the light she asks us to behold is the "blazing fire" in his eyes. And Billy Graham likewise urges us to understand that the loving, peaceful Christ and the flame-setting, sword-bearing Christ are not at odds. Grappling with Jesus' declaration, "I have come to bring fire on the earth" (Luke 12:49 NIV), Graham commends John Wesley's paraphrase, "I come to spread the fire of heavenly love over all the earth."

Other pieces in this collection helpfully reflect not only on the wonder of the light himself, but also on all that we can see *by* the light—including and especially our call as followers of the risen Christ to reflect his light by caring for the poor and the oppressed.

As we read *A Light Has Dawned*, we might envision this collection of reflections as a series of frames in a slow-motion sunrise. Each day of Advent and Christmastide, there is an invitation to allow the wonders of the incarnation to dawn on us incrementally, as we take in the light at a rate we can absorb. Imagine what might happen if we really do go slow this year. Can we, like Mary, learn to treasure the miracle, to ponder it in our hearts? Will we, like the Magi, train our eyes on the light and pursue it at any cost?

A Light Has Dawned is arranged to bring us through Advent and into Christmastide, culminating on January 6 with Epiphany. My prayer for you—and for me—is that by the time we reach those early days of January, we will have absorbed enough of the light to be able to say with Helmut Thielicke: "There is a sun 'that smiles at me,' and I can run out of the dark house of my life into the sunshine."

The Christ child, writes Harold John Ockenga, "was to be the shining light that would dawn in human hearts over the whole of the earth." We can rest assured that he will continue to dawn in our hearts, too. After all, "the darkness of nineteen [now twenty!] centuries has not been able to overcome that light, nor can the darkness of evil forces today extinguish the light of hope, faith, and love kindled by the coming of Jesus Christ."

Let it dawn on us

Like the morning sun

Let it chase our night away

Let it dawn on us

This is God with us

In the light of Christmas day[1]

---

1. From the song "Dawn on Us" by Carolyn Arends, © Running Arends Music/ASCAP.

✶

Advent

Alice Slaikeu Lawhead

On the first Sunday in December, I sit in Saint Aldate's church in Oxford and hear these words:

Now is the time to wake out of sleep: for now our salvation is nearer than when we first believed.

And I think: now is the time to make a purposeful trip to the supermarket and do the shopping for all the baking that needs to be done. Now is the time to make sure all the church programs and neighborhood parties and school activities are penciled in on the calendar so we don't overbook like we did last year. Now is the time to get up in the attic and dig out the Christmas decorations!

Now is the time to get the children to the barber, and call the university to see if they have any decent tickets left for this year's performance of *A Christmas Carol*.

Mrs. Williams has stepped to the lectern for the New Testament reading. I hear her proclaiming something about dates and times, my friends, and how we know perfectly well that the Day of the Lord comes like a thief in the night, and I wonder why it is that Christmas so often comes like a thief in the night for me.

I remember standing by my mother's side in the kitchen—on a little chrome stool to help me gain counter height—receiving patient instruction on how to form the small, savory meatballs that will be served at our Christmas Eve smorgasbord; how to work the cookie press as we prepare dozen upon dozen buttery spritzes that will melt in the mouth; how to heat the oil "just so" for puffy rosettes, and then dust them with powdered sugar. I can hear the slam of the back door as my father enters the kitchen and gives my mother a hug; she complains that she's behind on the baking, the whole thing has snuck up on her, and he steps back and asks, "What, you weren't expecting Christmas to be on the twenty-fifth this year? You thought maybe it would be later?"

Watch at all times, praying for the strength to stand with confidence before the Son of Man.

On the second Sunday of Advent I arrive at church having made my seasonal list, having reconciled the various programs and invitations, having done the big shopping trip. And the minister opens the service with:

The kingdom of God is close at hand: Repent, and believe the gospel.

Christmas is close at hand! Only ... only 16 more days 'til Christmas. Advent is short this year—always happens when Christmas comes in the middle of the week. I may never get the hang of Advent, I despair. It's not really in my blood. It's not a Baptist sort of concept, really. I was raised in a church that marked the seasons with observances like Valentine's Day Sunday, and Mother's Day Sunday, when we sang "Faith of Our Mothers" and an orchid corsage was given to the oldest mother, the mother with the most children present, and the mother who traveled the greatest distance. Or my favorite: Labor Day Sunday. On Labor Day Sunday, my dentist ushered us to our seats in that white smock he wore when he cleaned my teeth, the one that buttoned off-center and had such a high, almost Oriental collar. The farmers wore overalls to church, and women worshiped in house-dresses with pretty aprons. Businessmen and teachers looked the way they always did. Memorial Day flowers and special music, Thanksgiving Day prayers, New Year's Eve watchnight services—these composed the liturgical year of my childhood.

I am struck with free-church panic, the same sort of panic I get when I arrive for worship on Easter realizing that I'm not prepared for the Resurrection because I didn't observe Lent. My heart actually starts to thump, and I realize that I'm here, in his holy place, smack dab in the middle of Advent, and I don't have any idea what I'm supposed to be doing about it. What does it mean? What does it mean that the kingdom of God is close at hand? Repent, and believe the gospel—that's what it means.

I fall on my knees and confess my sins. "For the sake of your Son Jesus Christ, who died for us, forgive us all that is past; and grant that we may serve you in newness of life to the glory of your name. Amen," I intone with profound shame. Amen. How sweet are the words of the Lord to the taste, sweeter than honey to the mouth. Through his precepts we get understanding.

Third Sunday in Advent:

When the Lord comes, he will bring to light things now hidden in darkness, and will disclose the purposes of the heart.

When the Lord comes. My thoughts are back in time, 9 years ago and 11 years ago, when I was waiting for a child to be born. The anticipation! What a frightening, exciting time it was. Every morning I would waken and wonder: Is it today? Is this the day when the child will arrive? Is this the day when the child, hidden in my body, will be disclosed to me? When I see his hair, or her toes; his pointy head, her scrawny legs? I wanted so badly to know if I would be mother to a boy or a girl. Would the child be whole? Would it look like me, or Steve? My daytime thoughts were hopeful and expectant. But at night I had frightening dreams of deformity and death.

And when it came time for me to be delivered of my children, I was ready. There was no complaining that the babies arrived too soon. By the time my 140 pounds of body weight had become an alarming 185 pounds, by the time my feet no longer fit into my shoes, by the time I had attended three baby showers, I was ready. The apostle Paul had it right when he spoke of the Messiah's coming:

We know that the whole creation has been groaning as in the pains of childbirth right up to the present time.

The Scripture is being read now. "In the wilderness, prepare the way of the Lord, make straight in the desert a highway for our God." And I know that in my heart I am groaning with pain, panting for the kingdom, longing for justice and reconciliation.

Our Lord says, Surely I come quickly. Even so: come, Lord Jesus!

On the Fourth Sunday of Advent, I stand with the congregation for the introductory sentence.

The glory of the Lord shall be revealed: and all mankind shall see it.

My sons have been shaking the packages already under the Christmas tree. Grandma sent a big box of goodies to our overseas home via air mail—such extravagance! It arrived on Friday: a big, heavy box of toys and books and all manner of heavy gifts, flown from her town in the middle of the United States to our village in Britain. No forward planning, no thought given to cost, no wondering if it's "worth it." Out of the depth of her loving heart she had showered us with large and small gifts, several for each one of us. And now each individually wrapped parcel has found a place under our tree, and the children are wild with excitement. Ross complains of stomach aches and can hardly eat his meals. Drake has nervous legs; his body shakes at the dinner table. They've identified a jigsaw puzzle, and two books—those were easy. Ross was squeezing one small package, and it responded by playing an electronic melody. He and Drake laughed until they cried. A pocket video game! It had to be.

On Christmas morning all will be revealed. There have been hints that we might open gifts—at least one gift?—on Christmas Eve. That's Ross's proposal. But in his heart of hearts he doesn't want a preview. He doesn't want a little bit now and the rest later. He wants it all, in one huge, early-morning revelation.

I am sitting on an uncomfortable pew in a church where believers have worshiped since Elizabethan times. In this very spot, men and women of great faith and very little faith have gathered to worship, to pray, to proclaim with their presence that their hope is in the Lord. They, like me, have looked for the glory of the Lord to be revealed.

On this morning we pray for the needs of the world, for we have young men and women preparing for war in a distant land. We pray for the needs of the nation, for there is recession and unemployment and homelessness everywhere. We pray for the needs of our church, for we have a mission to fulfill. And we pray for ourselves, our marriages and our children and our friends. We pray for the glory of the Lord to be revealed.

We are waiting for an infinite God, unbound by time and space, to reveal himself to us in a way we can understand.

The virgin is with child and will soon give birth to a son: and she will call him Emmanuel, God-is-with-us.

On Christmas Eve, there is a service of lessons and carols. We begin our worship with a startling promise:

In the morning you shall see the glory of the Lord.

It's all come down to this. All the preparations—the cookies that were made, and the ones that weren't. The presents that were bought, and those that were forgotten.

The parties attended, the invitations declined. The cards sent and received, the prayers spoken and unspoken, the days of hectic activity and the quiet evenings staring at the fire. The shops are closed, the readying is over. If it hasn't been done yet, it won't be done at all. In the morning we shall see the glory of the Lord.

In the candlelit silence, eyes closed, I see a clearing. It is a small patch of nothing in particular, just a bit of nothingness in my world of cinnamon bread and carol sheets and pirate Legos. It is noteworthy for being uncluttered, as a small clearing in a deep wood is noteworthy for being without trees. It is a place of calm in my life, an unstructured center where schedules and deadlines and obligations cannot thrive. It's not much, but for me it's a start.

The uneven ground shall become level, and the rough places a plain.

It is Christmas Eve. I am almost faint with exhaustion and revelation.

The glory of the Lord shall be revealed, and all mankind shall see it.

✦

Drive-Through Christmas

Stanley Grenz

"*On the first day of Christmas my true love gave to me.*" Tony Bennett's voice wove its subtle magic throughout the shopping mall. "How appropriate," I thought, as I watched the shoppers scurry from store to store. The advertisements promised "just the right gifts at just the right price," allowing us to "give like Santa and save like Scrooge."

As I listened, I was struck with how we have turned Christmas around—not so much by commercializing the season, but through something deeper. Our McWorld of drive-through expectations has replaced patient waiting, followed by heartfelt joyous celebration, with the idolatry of instant gratification. This is poignantly evident in the fusillade of renditions of "The Twelve Days of Christmas" to which we are subjected this time of year.

The ancient Western church devised a rhythmic cycle for the celebration of Christ's incarnation. At the center was Advent, the 20-plus days beginning on the fourth Sunday before Christmas Day. By fasting and abstaining from public festivities, Christians were to prepare for the holy day by being drawn into the sense of longing for Messiah's coming felt by generations of God's faithful people.

This heightened sense of anticipation would, in turn, give way to overwhelming joy and festive celebration when Christmas Day finally came. Only then followed the 12 days of Christmas, climaxing on January 6 with Epiphany, the commemoration of the visit of the Magi.

As members of the fast-food generation, we have become so eager to get to Christmas that we bypass Advent. Whereas our forebears enjoined fasting and reflection, we try to enjoy days filled with more Christmas festivities than we can endure. Christmas has displaced Advent on our calendars.

But our bypassing of Advent runs deeper—altering our attitude to the story of Christ's birth. We know how the story ends. Knowing the end of the story so well, we want to rush through the long and tortuous details of how God prepared a people—of how "God sent his Son ... when the time had fully come" (Gal. 4:4 NIV). Rather than entering into the sense of expectation lying at the foundation of the narrative of Christ's entrance into the human plot-line, we read only the story's glorious climax. Rather than savoring the plaintive mood of "O Come, O Come Emmanuel," we immediately want to hear a robust version of "Joy to the World, the Lord Is Come." In short, we have our Christmas early and create a drive-through Christmas.

The irony of our situation is that in our rush toward Christmas, we end up truncating the celebration. Once December 25 is past, so is the holiday. Stretching the 12 days of Christmas until January 6 seems entirely out of place. In fact, we have eliminated the need to do so by moving the adoration of the Magi to our early Christmas: we efficiently (and ahistorically) place the wise men at the manger next to the shepherds. We cannot even stretch Christmas to December 26, for Boxing Day entices us to take our unwanted, reboxed gifts back to the stores or to buy boxes of the sale goods that draw us out in droves for one of the biggest shopping days of the year.

So we have our twelve-plus days of Christmas, just like the song says. But in our impatience born from the lure of instant gratification, we have transposed them. Christmas now precedes December 25. This may allow us to avoid the stressful waiting, the longing expectation and the forlorn cry of our forebears. But it also precludes us from sharing the exuberant joy of that first Christmas, for we cannot truly sing "Joy to the World" unless we have thoroughly rehearsed "O Come, O Come Emmanuel."

✺

The Poverty of Christmas

Katelyn Beaty

We don't believe in Christmas anymore.

We believe in Christmas gatherings, Christmas shopping, and Christmas recitals, of course, and even Christmas outreach events and Christmas acts of charity. If you are reading this issue of CT while fighting tryptophan-induced sleep, you know that Christmas has dominated our mass-mediated imagination since before Halloween. Christmas is the *piece de resistance* of a year spent hustling from one "big event" to another, anticipating the next holiday as we try to enjoy the present one.

Christmas is the biggest celebration on the calendar. But we know not what we celebrate.

Church leaders are in a major bind with this one. They have to compete with the usual rivals—Santa Claus, TV specials, and generic holiday cheer that can be felt without taking the family to a church. This year, Christian leaders face the allure of the new *Star Wars*. In a tossup between the baby Jesus and Luke Skywalker, I'm not sure most Christians would bet on the Christ Child over the Jedi Fighter.

In an effort to capture their neighbors' flitting attention, churches have perfected their Christmastime marketing game. It's no longer the Christmas sermon; it's four weeks of "Unwrapping Christmas" or "An Upside-Down Christmas," with children's programs and four weekend services—all requiring members' time and energy—to match. In a 2011 *Charisma* article on "the 12 mistakes of Christmas outreach," the No. 1 mistake is "not planning for something great." Even God knows you gotta have a WOW moment: "The Incarnation was one of God's Biggest Ideas," write the authors. "Create a new Christmas tradition, that of birthing new, remarkable ideas."

The Advent Conspiracy, founded in 2006 to encourage worship, simplicity, and giving, rightly draws the holiday away from ourselves, onto God and others. But even it tries to add big ideas—generosity and justice—to God's Big Idea. Our critiques of Christmas consumerism come wrapped in the packaging of a consumerist society.

It's like we don't trust the Incarnation to sell itself.

And maybe that's our problem. The trick about the Incarnation—God becoming *man; God* becoming man—is that it can't be sold, scheduled, or enjoyed in the way a glass of eggnog or a new gadget can. It refuses to bend to the rules of the market. It can only be beheld.

The story is found in Luke 2. A decree goes out. Joseph travels with Mary to the city of David, called Bethlehem, to be registered in Caesar's census. Then the text simply says: "And she gave birth to her firstborn, a son. She wrapped him in cloths and placed him in a manger, because there was no guest room available for them" (v. 7).[2] Such little fanfare, we might miss the pre-existent divine Son of God lying as a babe in a feeding trough.

---

2. Scripture quotations in this article are from the New International Version.

The plot doesn't pick up until the shepherds arrive to gaze upon the child whom the angel has foretold. When the shepherds find the baby, "they spread the word concerning what had been told them about this child" (v. 17) and go home praising God for all they have seen.

The passage in Luke returns us to the humility and poverty of the Christmas story. God does not enter our world donning bells and whistles, hoping to compete with Luke Skywalker or *Love Actually* reruns. He doesn't hope to "attract" more people with his "message." Instead, he waits for our eyes to adjust to the dim light emanating from the manger, to come, to see, to behold—and to truly celebrate.

This is very good news for church leaders, who experience great pressure at Christmas to increase attendance and giving. It means they need not think up a "big idea" to add to the Incarnation, but rather communicate—as clearly and plainly as possible—the big idea that is the Incarnation. Essayist Dorothy Sayers helps us on this point:

> It is the dogma that is the drama—not beautiful phrases, nor comforting sentiments, nor vague aspirations to loving-kindness and uplift, nor the

promise of something nice after death—but the terrifying assertion that the same God who made the world, lived in the world and passed through the grave and gate of death.

The Christmas story is "terrifying" because it is beyond human thought. It is nothing we humans could have invented. Yet it is everything that we need to hear in order to flourish in our dark and violent world. It is the great rescue plan of God, initiated before time itself to save sinners from death. It is salvation.

Come and behold.

☆

Bethlehem on a Budget

Tim Stafford

Budget time in my church comes during the approach of Christmas, for our fiscal year begins January 1. The juxtaposition is simply jarring.

Christmas in church is the dreamiest of times, when we rejoice in song as we never do otherwise, when the staunchest of iconoclasts welcome at least some decoration (a few pine boughs, perhaps) into the sanctuary, when our memories of childhood get tangled with the story of the birth of Jesus. That story has proven its strength to rekindle people's deepest hopes, whether they believe it or not. We who do believe it almost burst with hope at Christmastime.

But then we face the budget, the antithesis of the star atop the Christmas tree. The budget embodies dreary materialism, with all its inevitable disappointments. It is hard to synchronize this with Christmas; hard to harmonize the reedy sound of children practicing "Silent Night" with the anguished comments of the small committee of tired elders working late into the night to make the numbered columns come out right.

Not that budgets are entirely uninspiring. At my church, we begin the process in various committees by seeing visions and dreaming dreams. The Christian education committee envisions buying a complete library of Christian videos. The outreach and membership committee (with the pastor's enthusiastic concurrence) dreams of hiring a retired pastor to call on the sick and homebound. For the plant committee, paradise would be a repaved parking lot.

Ordinary though our dreams may sound, they are offspring of a wider vision: to live and proclaim the good news of Jesus Christ. When we work through the logistics of making our dreams come true, our dreams grow sharper. We are lifted out of our routines and, almost inevitably, inspired. We begin not merely to wish, but to hope.

But it is hard to transfer that hope to a budget. Most people grow weary just looking over the relentless columns of numbers. The budget categories ("operating expenses," "capital debt") speak openly as a clam; the figures bury intelligence in an avalanche of facts. The mind grows numb. Five minutes after beginning a budget confab, a $48.83 item seems as important as one costing $48,483.83. That is why people talk so much about "the bottom line." Above the bottom line grows an impenetrable jungle.

Yet we try. We dream our budgets and then present our dreams, carefully wrapped in numbers and logic, to the congregation. Members fill out pledge cards, and we who are designated leaders use those pledges to decide what we can do and what we cannot. Every year, our dreams are returned to us in pledge-sized fragments. We are given the money to do a few new things, but not half of what we dreamed.

So we will make do. And then try to forget it as we sing Christmas carols.

Last year, however, as I read the Christmas story and worked on the budget, a different perspective came to me, for the original Christmas was also a make-do affair.

There was, first, the matter of explaining the unexpected pregnancy. Joseph and Mary, Zechariah and Elizabeth knew the truth, but how could they make their neighbors believe it? Perhaps only God's opinion really counts, but judging from my own experience, those who love God still care what their neighbors think.

Then came the incredibly inconvenient summons to Bethlehem. When you are about to have a baby, you want relatives around to help. You desperately want your own home and your own things. Joseph and Mary made do in a crowded, strange town.

They could not even find a proper room. They had to make do with a stable, making a baby's bed out of whatever was at hand. No number of angel visitations could take away the wearying inconvenience of that lonesome birth. Surely this was not their dream—neither their dream of a first son, nor their dream of welcoming a Savior.

Yet it was in those make-do circumstances that God came. We truly sing of that baby in his thrown-together bed, "The hopes and fears of all the years are met in thee tonight."

To each of us a task is given. They had to watch their neighbors' eyes grow skeptical as they heard the circumstances of the pregnancy; I have to try convincing a dubious congregation that the extra money is really needed. They made do with a room paved in sheep dung; I may make do with a potholed parking lot. Neither situation seems to have much to do with the glory of God. Yet both sets of circumstances may welcome and nurture new, supernatural life. It happens particularly when we respond like Mary: "I am the Lord's servant. May it be to me as you have said."

It is the glory of God to conceal a matter, Proverbs tells us. In Bethlehem he concealed his Son in a manger. In my church he conceals his gospel in the budget. Often God fulfills our hopes in such ways, which seem in their untidiness to mock our hopes. How silently, how silently, the wondrous gift is given.

✵

Away from the Manger

Mary Ellen Ashcroft

Brace yourself, and I'll tell you about my Christmas idea. You've seen Advent calendars—they've got little doors with numbers on them, and, say for number 8, the flap is in a chimney and when you open it, there's a little owl perched inside. Or you flip up the top of a box (held by a little girl and marked 13) and there is a teddy bear with a red ribbon around its neck. Finally, of course, you swing open the big flaps (always number 24) and there is Jesus in a manger, snoozing away safely.

These calendars exist, of course, because it is so hard for kids to believe that Christmas is really coming—plus the fact that they need to keep track of how many days until they hit the jackpot under the Christmas tree.

They're helpful, but miss half of Advent's purpose: those first 24 days of December are not only supposed to help us remember Jesus' first advent as a baby, but also his second advent as Judge of the world. So, I suggest a Second Advent calendar.

The Book of Revelation provides most of the material. I'd want to start out the month low-key, like First Advent calendars do. The first day or two, when on your First Advent calendar you'd be opening a little oven door and finding a gingerbread man, the Second Advent calendar would feature the pale horse, being ridden by Death, with Hades following close behind (Rev. 6:8). Things would obviously need to heat up, and by the eleventh we would have trumpets heralding hail and fire mixed with blood (8:7). The fourteenth would give us the huge mountain all ablaze that would be thrown into the sea (8:8), and by the seventeenth we would have the locusts with stings like scorpions (9:3). Eventually (about the twentieth?), we would get to the war in heaven—Michael and his angels versus the great dragon (12:7–8). That would leave us a few days for the beast (complete with horns, etc.) and the scene with blood as high as the horses' bridles (14:20).

We could produce a version for pre-, post-, and amillennialist believers. But there is one thing that would be the same on the Second Advent calendar, despite your eschatological stance. That would be the image of Christ.

No helpless, snoozy baby here—this Jesus would be Christ in majesty, as he is described in Revelation 19: "His eyes are like blazing fire, and on his head are many crowns. He has a name written on him that no one but he himself knows. ... Out of his mouth comes a sharp sword with which to strike down the nations. ... He treads the winepress of the fury of the wrath of God Almighty. On his robe and on his thigh he has his name written: KING OF KINGS AND LORD OF LORDS" (VV. 12–16 NIV).

Imagine our Advent if it were this Jesus who was emblazoned on our consciousness. We can tiptoe past the drowsy baby as we buy stocking stuffers for little Susannah or an electric lint remover for Aunt Phyllis, forgetful of African children dying, bellies swollen and flies swarming around their eyes. But it would be ridiculous to try to sneak past this Jesus, his eyes aflame. We would squirm when we gave a cute Christmas mug (penguins in red-and-green top hats) to Betty at work—we'd keep waiting for just the right opportunity to tell her about Christ—knowing she would face those blazing eyes one day.

God knew we needed the Incarnation; he sent Emmanuel, "God with us." Our problem is that we want to keep Jesus as a baby, not have him swinging cords around temples and tastelessly knocking over tables.

It is not odd that we prefer the slumbering babe to the consuming fire: babies can be taken anywhere. Christmas last year brought a "Christian" version of "The Twelve Days of Christmas." Instead of the "partridge in a pear tree," we have the baby—"a child born to set the world free." Instead of "five golden rings," the chorus sweetly holds "five shopping malls." We can cart the infant Christ to a shopping mall, where he is as "at home" as an Easter bunny. But we wouldn't want to try that with Jesus as judge.

Long before Second Advent calendars, there were other devices to remind Christians of Christ's impending judgment. Peasants or nobles entering one of Europe's cathedrals saw a huge carved tympanum above their heads, which, throughout the Romanesque period, portrayed either Christ in Majesty or the Last Judgment. A Christ figure with wide, penetrating eyes dominates the tympanum. At Christ's right hand the blessed worship

Christ; on his left, the souls of the damned struggle with terror from a devouring "hell-mouth." Contemporary advertisers say to us of luxury, "Go ahead. You deserve it." But medieval sculptors pictured luxury as a vile snake, consuming its victims even as it draws them toward hell. Above the tympanum at Conques, France, a poem describes the joys of the blessed, the punishments of the damned, and ends with a warning: "Sinners, if you do not change your ways, know that a hard judgment will be upon you."

This Christ, not only mediator but also dreaded judge, dominated people's thinking throughout the Renaissance. Shakespeare's plays frequently reflect his characters' awareness of judgment. Clarence addresses his would-be assassins in *Richard III* (act I, scene iv), not advising them that their behavior is inappropriate or unkind, but that "the deed you undertake is damnable," and later, " ... For he holds vengeance in his hands / To hurl upon their heads that break his law."

Perhaps we would be more attracted to the idea of judgment if we were not so comfortable. If we huddled in our hut as Viking raiders burned the rest of our village, dragging our children into waiting boats; if we felt the lash of a whip across our sweating, bleeding flesh as we crossed the Atlantic in a slaver, we would be more likely to echo Milton:

Rise, God, judge thou the earth in might,
This wicked earth redress,
For Thou art he who shall by right
The Nations all possess.

We may not long for judgment, but somewhere inside us we believe in it. We don't like the idea of a Nazi war criminal eating lobster thermidor in a fine restaurant and living on the French Riviera. Robin Hood appeals to us because he robs from the rich and gives to the poor, and tricks that nasty, usurping Prince John. We like to see villains get punished—like wicked stepmothers who always get their just deserts, and dragons that are finally slain by noble knights.

We are even willing to bring judgment closer to home, and tolerate God's wrath on gamblers, pornographers, and drug dealers. Our real hesitation is with judgment on ourselves. We don't dwell on the times we act like wicked stepmothers (in the privacy of our homes, or with windows rolled up, as we denounce "those stupid drivers"). What about our dragonish thoughts as we recline comfortably on our hoard and others die of starvation? We would rather not take literally Jesus' words: "There is nothing concealed that will not be disclosed, or hidden that will not be made known. What you have said in the dark will be heard in the daylight, and what you have whispered in the ear in the inner rooms will be proclaimed from the roofs" (Luke 12:3).[3]

We try to leave him neatly tucked in the manger, but Jesus as judge may haunt us. A Christian woman told me about her luxury cruise: "The ship had teak decks, two pools, a Jacuzzi, elegant lounges and staterooms. There were sumptuous brunches on deck and dinners with silver and crystal, escargot and duck a l'orange. But when we got off the ship," she said, "there were children, hungry in rags, staring at us." Those staring eyes were to her the eyes of Jesus, the same blazing eyes we avoid when we spend an extra $20 on designer jeans, push past a bag lady (careful not to think of her as human), or turn quickly by the picture of the hungry five-year-old in a magazine. Malachi asks, "Who can endure the day of his coming? Who can stand when he appears? For he will be like a refiner's fire" (3:2).

---

3. Scripture quotations in this article are from the New International Version.

Advent is about getting ready, and Jesus tells many parables about readiness. The ten virgins are only judged wise or foolish by how ready they are to meet the bridegroom. The parable closes with a disturbing picture: virgins knocking on the door and pleading that it be opened. Jesus delivers his punch line: "Therefore, keep watch, because you do not know the day or the hour" (Matt 25:13).

How can we be ready and watching? Not by calculations or speculations. Certainly not by leaving Jesus safely snoozing in his crib while we shop, wrap presents, hang the wreath, and bake cookies. Peter poses and answers the question: "Since everything will be destroyed in this way, what kind of people ought you to be? You ought to live holy and godly lives as you look forward to the day of God and speed its coming" (2 Pet 3:11–12).

✧

Saved through Child-Bearing

Wendy Alsup

At first, amid the unmistakable crunch of steel and aluminum, I thought I was the victim. A pang of outrage, a twinge of self-pity. But it quickly dawned on me that I was the one who caused the accident.

I was responsible for the damage to a stranger's car. I had caused the stress the man in the other car endured. It was a relatively minor accident, but I still felt the weight of the loss I'd caused both of us. And there was something more than embarrassment and anxiety. There was shame. I felt a specific form of indignity for being a *woman* who had hit a *man's* car.

In Saudi Arabia, women have only just been granted the right to vote. But they still aren't allowed to drive vehicles. Even countries that consider such limitations archaic often hold steadfast to the stereotype of women as bad drivers. It can be a self-fulfilling belief: studies show that these kinds of negative stereotypes actually affect women's confidence while driving.

I want to prove myself as helpful and responsible, not flighty and negligent. I want to be the person who keeps an accident from happening, not the one who causes it. But I had caused it. Was I really a bad driver? Was I merely fearful of being labeled one because of my gender? Either way, the crash filled me with shame.

Like many women before me, I felt both legitimate and illegitimate shame. Like the first woman in the Garden of Eden, I felt the shame of genuine failure. But I also felt the impact of a lingering shame projected onto Eve by Adam, who blamed her for his eating the fruit. Ever since the events of the Fall, women have felt both sides of shame.

At Christmastime, we tend to focus on God's deliverance of the righteous from illegitimate shame. The Virgin Mary experiences what seems to everyone else to be a shameful pregnancy, and even Joseph, who "did not want to expose her to public disgrace … had in mind to divorce her quietly." But she is justified by an angel of the Lord, who puts the story right, and by all later generations who call her blessed.

But there is another biblical Christmas story that reminds us that the Christ child came to take away not only our illegitimate shame, but all of it. Ironically, it is a verse that many women prefer to avoid from fear that it just adds more shame: "But women will be saved through childbearing—if they continue in faith, love and holiness with propriety" (1 Tim 2:15).[4]

This statement has challenged even those with a robust faith in the God of the Bible. But it's a Christmas story indeed. It's not the story of Mary and Joseph. Nor the story of Mary and Elizabeth. It's the Christmas story of Mary and Eve.

The first woman was created in the image of God, a helper suitable for the man, to work together with him to fulfill God's creation mandate. There was no architecture or art, no fine foods or engineering marvels. This lack was part of their mandate. God tasked Adam and Eve with moving into his creation to steward it and rule over it, to

---

4. Scripture quotations in this article are from the New International Version.

create in his image from the foundation he left them. It was a clear and noble calling. Eve's story starts with glory.

But it seems to end in humiliation. Eve allowed Satan to tempt her away from trust in God's plan and purposes. She disobeyed God's only command and played an instrumental part in the fall of man and warping of creation as a result. Adam then blamed Eve, seeking to distract from the fact of his presence with her when it happened.

God didn't join Adam in the blame. Instead, he condemned the serpent:

> "Because you have done this, cursed are you above
> all livestock and all wild animals! You will crawl
> on your belly and you will eat dust all the days of
> your life. And I will put enmity between you and
> the woman, and between your offspring and hers;
> he will crush your head, and you will strike his heel"
> (Gen 3:14–15).

God shifts Adam's blame from Eve to Satan with the clarifying words "because *you* have done this." Eve had been captured by Satan, ensnared to do his will. Meanwhile, Adam stood by and watched it all happen.

God curses Satan in a specific way: by placing him at war with the woman. He promises to put enmity—hostility or warfare—between Satan and the woman and between Satan's offspring and hers. Her seed, the fruit of her womb who would be nourished at her breast, would strike Satan with a knockout blow.

God speaks words of redemption in Eve's presence before he announces the painful consequences of the Fall in her relationships. Rather than merely offering Eve the personal hope of her own rescue from her sin, God speaks of her as the vessel through which would come the salvation of all. Woman may have taken part in the Fall, but she would also nurture in her womb and at her breast the one who would save us all from the Fall. Eve's shame would be reversed through the coming of the Savior.

In 1 Timothy 2, the apostle Paul instructs Timothy in matters of the local church, including the role of women. In a particularly controversial passage, Paul recounts Adam and Eve's story, making an argument that has caused many readers to cringe: "And Adam was not the one deceived; it was the woman who was deceived and became a sinner. But women will be saved through childbearing—if they continue in faith, love and holiness with propriety" (1 Tim 2:14–15).

This passage is perplexing at first glance. Is Paul looking at woman's role in the Fall and cruelly rubbing it in? Is he arguing that women are saved through the act of having children? Is he arguing for a peculiar kind of works-based religion? Is he referring to the woman's unique ability to develop image-bearers in her womb, an inherent safety net for humanity in the face of the possibility of annihilation?

In fact, Paul's words parallel nicely with God's own words to Satan and Eve after the Fall. When Paul uses the word "saved through childbearing," he is not referring to the physical survival of humanity through procreation, but to the birth of the Child, literally "*the* Childbirth," as William Mounce and John Stott have pointed out in their respective commentaries. The Greek use of a definite article that points to the unique, one and only nature of this childbirth, and the larger context of the discussion of Eve in the Garden in the previous two verses, bring us full circle to God's prophecy: Through the woman would come the Savior who would defeat Satan. She would be saved, or redeemed, through the birth of *the* Child.

God told Satan immediately after the Fall that he would be at war with woman; history has borne out that truth. Even today, in many impoverished areas of the world, the mere words "it's a girl" can be deadly. The female gender continues to be systematically devalued and abused, with sex-selective abortions and infanticide regularly resulting in female deaths.

Because the woman was the vessel through which God would bring his Son and our salvation into the world, she became one of Satan's most hated enemies. She may have opened the gate that let in the enemy, but she also bore the One who would close it permanently. While she had been the one that Satan first approached as an ally in his plan to bring down God's perfect creation, Satan would be at war with her forevermore because her seed would ultimately defeat him.

But first there was another woman: Mary. You may have seen the iconic image of Mary consoling Eve. Painted in 2003 by a sister at Mississippi Abbey in Iowa, it was later made into a Christmas card, and last year went viral on the Internet. Mary, her womb swollen with the Christ child, gently cups the face of dejected Eve, who rests her hand on Mary's belly. I cried when I saw it, moved by the hope offered to Eve as she endured the shame and consequences of her own choices.

But the marvelous thing about the consolation of Eve is that it was God himself, not Mary, who spoke of the role her gender would play in the ultimate defeat of Satan. She had been entrusted with the fate of humanity once and failed, but God would entrust woman with the fate of humanity yet again. The Child would be born from her womb, nourished at her breast, and sheltered in her arms. This salvation would be demonstrated, according to 1 Timothy, by her perseverance in faith, love, and holiness.

Though some elevate Mary to sinless perfection, the reality is that she simply trusted and obeyed God in her defining moment. A sinner herself, she bore into the world the One who would never sin. He bore her sin and ours. And he bore Eve's shame and ours. Eve, Mary, and all who believe between and after them are saved through the birth of this child.

This Christmas, as we meditate on the incarnation of Christ, we can marvel at the ways Jesus' coming was inextricably tied to the woman. While our need for salvation may be tied to Eve, the birth of the Savior is tied to Mary. The shame of Eve finds its ultimate reversal in the dignity of Mary. Wherever Christ's name is received, woman is saved and her dignity restored, as God himself foretold over Eve.

God's words over Eve were fulfilled in Mary, and the dignity of woman is in the deliverance of all mankind. The Savior has been born and the battle won. Through faith in him, we are rescued from both the legitimate and illegitimate shame of Eve. We are now heralds and participants of grace. Through the life and death of Christ, we are dignified, restored to glory, and empowered to fulfill God's purposes for us, just as we were created to be.

✧

Christmas in Afghanistan

Leigh C. Bishop

How strange, Lord, is your timing. Why, of all evenings, this evening?

It has been over a month since we stood at attention along the sides of this road, each waiting quietly, thoughtfully. Until tonight, one could almost imagine that peace had broken out somehow, and we were simply too busy to heed the good news, pack up, and go home. Now, the snow-covered mountain peaks that surround us are barely visible in the gathering gloom.

In the dusky dimness far to our right, the procession of military vehicles emerges onto the road and slowly approaches, passing between the ranks of a thousand or more soldiers, sailors, and airmen drawn up on either side of the asphalt strip for the Fallen Comrade Ceremony. The flag-draped steel casket is just visible from behind, as the open Humvee glides by and turns toward the tarmac to deliver its burden to a westbound C-17. Without command or signal, all salute as it passes.

Somewhere, a family has just learned that a son, a brother, is coming home from the war. A Christmas homecoming. But not as they had hoped.

Why, Lord, do you allow this time, of all times, to become for some a memorial of searing pain? To touch all future Christmas celebrations with a sadness that can never in a lifetime be entirely wiped away?

How often I have heard from patients and acquaintances, "I can't enjoy Christmas. Too many bad memories." For many, those memories are sullied by family conflicts, personal betrayals, alcohol-fueled rage. Or perhaps by nothing more than petty arguments about presents—gifts laid aside and forgotten long before the resentment died.

But this? This is something of an entirely different order: the cost of freedom and duty all lovingly bound up in the wrapping of solemn military honors, and delivered on the night when angels sang to shepherds. Except tonight, the angels surrounding Bagram are silent.

Or is it just that we are too dull of heart to hear them?

For if the hope of Christmas is not sufficient for this, it is sufficient for nothing. Surely it is those who mourn—the wounded and the downtrodden—for whom Christmas is especially intended. And for those for whom the holidays are a reminder of grief and poverty, for those who would just as soon do without it—if anything, we need more Christmas, not less. Not to drown our sorrows in contrived cheer, but to redeem and transform them.

We would be as those described by the prophet Isaiah: "The people walking in darkness have seen a great light; on those living in the land of the shadow of death a light has dawned" (9:2 NIV).

An hour later, I find myself walking along the same stretch of Disney Drive, the main avenue of Bagram Airfield. All is different. At the crossing known as Four Corners, soldiers holding candles are belting out Christmas carols with gusto. Down the street, luminarias brighten the walkway into the clamshell-shaped auditorium, where cheerful groups of uniformed men and women enter for a Christmas concert. Two blocks away, the chapel is filling for the six o'clock Christmas Eve service.

War, writes C. S. Lewis in the essay "Learning in War-Time," reveals a hunger in human beings for joy and meaning that will not be set aside for even the most difficult of circumstances. "They propound mathematical theorems in beleaguered cities, conduct metaphysical arguments in condemned cells, make jokes on scaffolds, discuss the last new poem while advancing to the walls of Quebec, and comb their hair at Thermopylae. This is not panache; it is our nature."

Jesus did not come just to provide an occasion to sing carols, drink toasts, feast, and exchange gifts. But we are right to do these things, even as soldiers die and families grieve, because he came. And in his coming, he brought joy and peace—the joy that overcomes our sorrows, and the only kind of peace that ultimately matters. It's the peace of which the end of all wars, terrible as they are, is merely one token. It's the peace that means the long war between the heart and its Maker is over. It's a peace treaty offered in Bethlehem and signed, in blood, on Calvary.

So, joy to the world, and to every celebrating or grieving or hurting soul in it. The Lord has come. Let heaven and nature—and even those who stand watch with lighted candles in the land of the shadow of death—sing.

Gift Wrapping God

Mary Ellen Ashcroft

We wreathe our doors with juniper and holly, deck our shrubs with tiny white lights and our living rooms with spruce trees, candles, Nativity scenes. We dress ourselves for Christmas: she sporting a cotton sweater with stars and snowflakes, he wearing a candy-caned tie, baby kicking green and red socks with tiny bells.

Ironic, all of this decking, when you consider that the Christmas movement of God is away from glitter and glory. To get ready for Christmas, God undressed.

God stripped off his finery and appeared—how embarrassing—naked on the day he was born. God rips off medals of rank, puts aside titles, honors, and talents, and appears in his birthday suit. *Veiled in flesh the Godhead see; hail the incarnate deity.* In the incarnation, things heavenly and earthly are gathered into one: one in the naked flesh and folds of God.

Do we get Santa Claus and God mixed up? We think of a portly God with a long white beard, well covered in red flannel and fur. It's part of our great project—clothing God—making him as respectable as we are. No shirt, no shoes, no service, we tell him. Dressing God is, for many, a compulsive hobby.

God deserves the best-dressed celebrity award, as we have robed God not only in Santa suits, but in fine marble, gilt, marvelous mosaic. Let God be anything but naked. Yes, I want that cloth right there: thank you, sculptors, for helping God where he could not help himself, covering God's bare flesh and unprotected love.

When the gospel was first preached, Romans laughed at the idea of a god become flesh. Oh, sure, a god might have a fling with a mortal woman and then disappear to better realms. But you know your side of the tracks, and the gods know theirs. God become flesh—hilarious!

Instead of laughing with the Romans, we've done a sleight of hand to turn the celebration of the incarnation into Christmas. Into the hat we stuff a fleshly God; out pops tinsel, wrapping paper, photos of children with starry eyes. The incantation? Hocus pocus backwards—no, this is not my body, not my blood. Because of this trick, many educated people know nothing of what scandalized the Romans.

Dig under stockings, Christmas concert programs, carols, a gingerbread house recipe, and—Oh my God. What is it? A baby. Not a silent symbol of benign blessing, but meconium, squalling cries, desperate need for warm breast, loving eyes to search his: God is naked and not ashamed.

God's heart of love moved him to make choices that seem absurdly unstrategic. If he'd kept his wits about him, God could have hit the ground running, birthed as an emperor or at least to wealth. A wise God would rub shoulders with movers and shakers, attend presidential prayer breakfasts, speak at the National Press Club. Even the Devil could see God was ill advised, and in the wilderness he offered Jesus the opportunity to pull rank. But Jesus declined. God trotted past the great and leapt onto lesser mortals, knocking them flat by his grace.

Over and over, God plays the fool. He sends the massed angel choir to a rabble of shepherds. Why send such a hard-to-book troupe to riffraff who would have been wowed by one shabby angel clutching a bit of tinsel? God over-the-top throws the party-to-end-all-parties for scum who had never been to so much as a kegger.

God doesn't care whether they are wearing Brooks Brothers or bathrobes; God prefers them smelling of sweat or pig, not Obsession or soap. God doesn't worry about proper accents, good grammar. God has hidden these things from the wise and revealed them to infants. Searching high for God in mystical experiences, complicated revelations, asceticism, spiritual exercises? God is laid low, tucked under the mundane. Look down, not up—dig to find the treasure buried in your own backyard, called flesh.

Three men—from noble families, midfifties, wise—seek exalted experience of God. Willing to travel. The wise men looked high (not low) until their necks were cricked. Dazzled by stars, they expect to be bedazzled by God. Looking up, they play a game with God: Hide the holy one, and God is "it." Check the palace, of course. Where else could God be? Many people spend their lives like those wise men, looking for God in exotic spiritual experiences, not realizing that the extraordinary truth is under their noses.

As evangelicals we have focused on the saving death of Christ but thrown out the incarnation in our Christmas wrappings. As we cover God with Christmas, we hide what is most distinctive about Christianity. And this is the tragedy: what many don't know about Christianity is that God has chosen to identify with their pain, their humanness, their flesh. This is what we've lost as we have exchanged the Feast of the Incarnation for Christmas.

As we have dressed God in his Christmas best, we have covered the jewel of the Christian faith—God's choice of flesh, of identification with humanity and therefore pain. The earliest Christmas hymns sing of incarnation; most Victorian ones hum harps of gold, reminding us over and over of straw and donkeys. We need to look for ways to communicate to unbelievers the wonderful news of a God who is unwilling to stand apart from us, who must become God with us.

Think about it. God could have chosen distance: contemplating from a detached, divine reverie, creating inanimate objects and slinging them around the universe. Or God could just be. He could have masked himself with the passive face of Buddha, gazing beyond pain.

Sometimes when I am confronted with terrible pain, I wish I were Buddhist so I could distance myself from the dust, flesh, and torment of the human condition.

But no, the face of God is spun with joy, drawn by pain, creased with greeting. God avoids realms of esoteric understanding, wandering instead into the mud of identification, the spit and dirt of costly involvement. In flesh we endure heat, cold, toothache; in flesh we fear the rapist, the cancer.

God could not be God-with-us if he wasn't flesh. The flesh of the baby is father to the flesh of the man. In his flesh, the spit of God mixed with the dirt of Galilee to make a healing paste. The naked baby must be flesh so that God can be stripped again, trading his dusty garments for the splinters of the cross.

No wonder we pile the Christmas tree skirt, the Christmas card list, the invitation to a Christmas party over the flesh-and-blood baby. Please, someone, load on the patchwork wreath, the felt stockings. Turn on somebody's Christmas tape. We don't want a God who becomes flesh.

The true Christmas story scares us spitless. If God undressed, we might have to join him—remove our self-sufficiency suits, pull off our health-and-well-being designer sweats. Perhaps instead of shopping we need to spend December reminding ourselves of God's choice of vulnerability and pondering its implications. Perhaps we need to call December 25th the Celebration of the Incarnation, to greet each other with incarnation greetings—instead of "Happy Holidays" or "Merry Christmas" we could shout, "God chose flesh!" "God became one of us!"

The Feast of the Incarnation is the time to dance to the descending scales of God's throwing off omnipotence. The Word was made flesh and dwelt among us—God closer than close. That's what we could be celebrating. This is the Christmas story as it should be told. This naked God is the path to God.

✴

Christmas Shame

Eugene H. Peterson

Two years ago at Christmas I was living in Montana in the Rocky Mountains where I grew up. The National Forest Service there allows people to cut their own Christmas tree. So Jan, my wife, and I went out one day with an axe into the snow-filled forest to get ours. We spotted what looked like the right tree—it was 200 yards up a hillside, and we had to tramp through snow to get to it. In that forest and on that hillside it was a spectacularly beautiful tree. But after we got it back to our home on the lake and set it up in our wood-fired and carpeted living room, we realized that a considerable amount of its charm had been lost in transit.

It was an Engleman spruce, a tree with character, having lived a hard life on the mountain, and we had hiked through 16 inches of snow to get it. It still looked handsome enough to me, but when our three children, all adults now, arrived to celebrate the holiday with us, they took one look and mocked.

They were used to coifed Scotch pines, bought from the Lions Club in the Safeway parking lot in Maryland. If those were too picked over, we patronized the Boy Scouts selling from the Methodist parking lot. Buying a tree was a family affair, with arguments about size and thickness and symmetry. This was our first tree chosen without the benefit of children.

In Montana, with an entire forest of trees to pick from, they thought we could have done better. We reminisced about the Christmas trees we had bought and set up and decorated. The more we talked, the more scrawny this Engleman spruce appeared. But finally we all agreed it was a tree, after all, and the moment it was designated Christmas tree it was suitable.

People worry these days about keeping Christ in Christmas; no one has any anxiety about keeping the tree in Christmas. Nobody I know discusses the pros and cons of the matter; it is simply done. There must be numerous households in America where no prayers are offered at Christmas, no carols sung, and no nativity story told. But there can be few households where there is no Christmas tree. The tree is required. We always had a tree, and always will. It is as much a part of Christmas as the crèche and "Silent Night."

But I do remember a Christmas when there was no tree. I was eight years old. My mother, an intense woman capable of fierce convictions, was reading the prophecy of Jeremiah and came upon words she had never noticed before:

Thus says the Lord:

"Learn not the way of the nations,
   nor be dismayed at the signs of the heavens
   because the nations are dismayed at them,
   for the customs of the peoples are false.
   A tree from the forest is cut down,
   and worked with an axe by the hands of a craftsman.
   Men deck it with silver and gold;
   they fasten it with hammer
   and nails
   so that it cannot move" (Jer 10:2–4 RSV).

There was no doubt in her mind that the Holy Spirit, through the prophet Jeremiah, had targeted our American Christmas in his warning satire. Every detail fit our practice.

A couple of weeks before Christmas, on a Sunday afternoon, my father would get the axe and check its edge. He was a butcher, used to working with sharp tools, and he did not tolerate dull edges. When I heard the whetstone applied to the axe, I knew that the time was near. We bundled into our Model A Ford pickup, my parents and baby sister and I.

If it was not too cold, I rode in the open truck bed with our springer spaniel, Brownie, and held the axe. It was a bouncy ride of ten miles to Lake Blaine, where the Swan Range of the Rocky Mountains took its precipitous rise from the valley floor. There had been a major forest fire in this region a few years before, so the trees were young—the right size to fit into our living room. I always got to pick the tree; it was a ritual I stretched out as long as parental patience and winter temperatures would accommodate.

My father then took over, swinging the axe. Four or five brisk cuts, and the green-needled spire was horizontal in the snow: *A tree from the forest is cut down.*

He then squared the base of the trunk so it would be easy to mount when we got it back home: *Worked with an axe by the hands of a craftsman.* My father was deft with the axe—the wood chips from the whittling released the fragrance of resin in the winter air.

When we arrived home, I climbed into the attic and handed down the box of decorations. We had multicolored lights on our tree, and lots of tinsel. Across the street, my best friends had all blue lights, and I felt sorry for them, stuck with a monochrome Christmas.

My father took slats from packing boxes that our sausage and lunch meats were shipped in—there was always a pile of these boxes in the alley behind our butcher shop—and cut them into four 18-inch supports and nailed them to the tree trunk: *They fasten it with hammer and nails so that it cannot move.*

By now it was late afternoon and dark. Our Douglas fir—it was always a Douglas fir for us, no other evergreen was a Christmas tree—was secure and steady before our living room window, facing the street. We strung the lights, hung the silver and gold ornaments, and draped the tinsel: *Men deck it with silver and gold.*

When we were done, I ran out onto the gravel road (the paving on Fourth Street West fell short by about 400 yards of reaching our house) and looked at it from the outside, the way passers-by would see it, the framed picture of our Christmas ritual adventure into and out of the woods. I imagined strangers looking at it and wishing they could be inside with us, part of the axe/Model A pickup/Lake Blaine/tree-choosing/tree-cutting/tree-mounting/tree-decorating liturgy that I loved so much.

And I would look across the street at the tree with blue lights where the Mitchell twins, Alva and Alan, lived—so cold and monotonous. They never went to church, and at times like this it showed. I couldn't help feeling privileged and superior, but also a little sorry for them: Christian pride modified by Christian compassion.

And then, in the winter of 1940, when I was eight years old, we didn't have a tree: *For the customs of the peoples are false.* It wasn't just the tree that was absent, the richly nuanced ritual was abolished. A noun, "tree," was deleted from December, but along with it an adjective, "Christmas." Or so I felt.

And it was all because Jeremiah had preached his Christmas Tree Sermon. Because Jeremiah had looked through his prophetic telescope, his Spirit-magnified vision reaching across 12,000 miles and 2,600 years saw in detailed focus what we did every December, and denounced it as idolatry. And it was because my mother cared far more about Scripture than culture.

I was embarrassed—humiliated was more like it—humiliated as only eight-year-olds can be humiliated. Abased. Mortified. I was terrified of what my friends in the neighborhood would think: They would think we were too poor to have a tree. They would think I was being punished for some unspeakable sin and so deprived of a tree. They would think we didn't care about each other and didn't have any fun in our house. They would feel sorry for us. They would feel superior to us.

As a regular feature of the child-world holiday socializing in our neighborhood, we went to each other's houses, looked at the presents under the trees, wondering what we would get. Every house was so different—I marveled at the odd ways people arranged their furniture. I was uneasy with the vaguely repellent odors in houses where the parents smoked and drank beer. At the Zacharys, three houses down, there was a big pot of moose-meat chili simmering on the back of the wood stove for most of the winter—it was easily the best-smelling house among my friends.

But that year, I kept everyone out of our house. I was ashamed to have them come in and see the bare, treeless room. I was terrified of the questions they would ask. I made up excuses to keep them out. I lied: "My sister has a contagious disease"; "My mother is really mad and I can't bring anybody in." But the fact of *no-Christmas-tree* could not be hidden. After all, it was always in our front window.

Alva and Alan, the twins who never went to church, asked the most questions, sensing something wrong, an edge of taunting now in their voices. I made excuses: "My dad is too busy right now; we're planning on going out next week." And on and on.

I was mostly terrified that they would discover the real reason we didn't have a tree: that God had commanded it (at least we thought so at the time)—a religious reason! But religion was the one thing that made us better than our neighbors; and now, if they were to find out our secret, it would make us worse!

My mother read Jeremiah to me and my little sister that year and talked about Jesus. She opened the Bible to the story of the nativity and placed it on the table where the Christmas tree always stood. I never told her how I felt, or what I knew everyone in the neighborhood was saying. I carried my humiliation secretly, as children often do, stoical in the uncomprehending adult world.

It is odd when I think back on it now, but we never went to church on Christmas. Every detail of our lives was permeated with an awareness of God. There was a rigorous determination to let Scripture and Christ shape not only our morals and worship, but also the way we used language and wore our clothes. Going to church was the act that pivoted the week. But there was no church-going on Christmas.

On Christmas Eve we exchanged and opened presents; on Christmas Day we had a dinner at our house with a lot of relatives in attendance, plus any loose people in the neighborhood—bachelors, widows, runaways.

Christmas dinner was full of Norwegian talk. It was the only day in the year I heard Norwegian spoken. My uncles and aunts reminisced over their Norway Christmases, and savored the sounds of their cradle tongue. The Christmas menu was always the same:

lutefisk, fish with all the taste and nutrients leached out of it by weeks of baptism in barrels of brine, and *lefsa,* an unleavened, pliable flat bread with the texture (and taste) of a chamois cloth.

There was a stout but unsuccessful attempt to restore flavor by providing great bowls of melted butter, salt cellars, and much sugar. It was a meal I never learned to like. But I loved the festivities—the stories in Norwegian that I couldn't understand, the laughter, the fun, the banter.

The primary source of the banter was my favorite uncle. He was the best storyteller and always seemed to have the most fun. He also posed as an atheist (I think it was a pose), which provoked my mother, on alternate days, to prayer and indignation. On the Christmas we had no tree, he surpassed himself in banter.

He was the first to remark its absence, and his remark was a roar: "Evelyn [my mother's name], where the hell is the Christmas tree? How the hell are we going to celebrate a Norwegian Christmas without a tree?" (He was also the only person I ever heard use profanity in our home, which set him apart in my child mind on a sort of craggy eminence.) My mother's reply, a nice fusion of prayer and indignation, was a match to his raillery:

"Brother, we are not celebrating a Norwegian Christmas this year; we are celebrating a Christian Christmas." Then she got out Jeremiah and read it to him. He was astonished. He had no idea that anything that tellingly contemporary could come out of an old-fashioned Bible. He was silenced, if only briefly.

The next year we had a Christmas tree. The entire ritual was back in place without explanation. Our gray and rust Model A was replaced by a red Dodge half-ton, but that was the only change. I never learned what authority preempted Jeremiah in the matter of the Christmas tree. Years later my mother occasionally said, "Eugene, do you remember that silliness about the Christmas tree when you were eight years old?" I didn't want to remember, and we didn't discuss it.

But now I want to remember. And I want to discuss it. It doesn't seem at all silly now. My mother died four years ago, and so I am not going to find out the details that interest me—the turns and twists of pilgrimage during those years when she was so passionate in pursuit of a holy life. She may have been wise in restoring the tree to our Christmas celebrations, but I am quite sure that it was not silliness that banned it that single year.

The feelings I had that Christmas when I was eight years old may have been the most authentically Christmas feelings I have ever had, or will have: the experience of humiliation, of being misunderstood, of being an outsider. Mary was pregnant out of wedlock. Joseph was an apparent cuckold. Jesus was born in poverty. God had commanded a strange word; the people in the story were aware, deeply and awesomely aware, that the event they were living was counter to the culture and issued from the Spirit's power.

They certainly experienced considerable embarrassment and inconvenience—did they also clumsily lie to their friends and make excuses at the same time they persisted in faith? All the joy and celebration and gift-receiving in the gospel nativity story took place in a context of incomprehension and absurdity. Great love was given and received and celebrated, a glorious festivity, but the neighborhood was not in on it, and the taunts and banter must have cut cruelly into their spirits.

So, Mother, thank you. And don't apologize for the silliness. Thank you for providing me with a taste of the humiliation that comes from pursuing a passionate conviction in Christ. Thank you for introducing into my spirit a seed of discontent with all cultural displays of religion, a seed that has since grown tree-sized. Thank you for being relaxed in grace and reckless enough to risk a mistake. Thank you for being scornful of caution and careless of opinion. Thank you for training me in discernments that in adult years have been a shield against the seduction of culture-religion. Thank you for the courage to give me Jesus without tinsel, embarrassing as it was for me (and also for you?).

Thank you for taking away the Christmas tree the winter I was eight years old. And thank you for giving it back the next year.

✨

Christmas on Tiptoe

Donald J. Shelby

In an aggressive bid to attract members, a Midwest megachurch recently sunk $25,000 into decorations for a lavish Christmas program. We've come a long way from the manger.

Something in us likes to be dazzled and entertained, to have our senses galvanized with spectacle. There are even public-relations firms that specialize in media blitzes and festive openers, providing clowns, fireworks, and dance troupes to showcase a new product or introduce an aspiring celebrity with great hoopla.

Why did God not use a few special effects when Jesus was born, and let loose a miracle or two like those that occurred at the dawn of Creation, or with Moses and the Exodus? Why did he not go for maximum exposure by choosing Athens, Rome, Alexandria—even Jerusalem—for Christ's birth? And if the prophet Isaiah had announced that the coming Messiah King, the virgin's child, would finally sit in royal splendor on David's throne, why a cave as the setting for the birth?

True, a star appeared, but not many knew why or for whom. And an angel chorus heralded the event, but none but a few poor shepherds heard their announcement. Surely *this* was not the auspicious beginning one would expect for the birth of the world's Savior.

Yet this anomaly tells us something. It points us not only to what God was up to then, but also how Jesus comes today into the midst of our lives.

Jesus came first to us, as preacher George Buttrick suggested, as a gentle sign. A working-class couple welcomes their first child in a stable with its pungent odors, among animals whose moist eyes reflect the flickering light of the oil lamps brought in for the birth. No sounding of trumpets, no marching of armies, no retinue of servants, just the quiet rustle of animals, the familiar human sounds heard at any birth, and the wail of a new baby who was then laid in a manger as his first crib. God "came down the backstairs at Bethlehem," wrote Buttrick, "lest he blind us by excess of light." He came first to a small town—Bethlehem—as a child who would beckon and enable, save and restore through the power of love.

It is no surprise, then, to see Jesus later calling his followers to gentle ways: "If any one strikes you on the right cheek, turn to him the other also. ... Love your enemies and pray for those who persecute you" (Matt 5:39, 44).[5] He also told them: "Blessed are the meek, for they shall inherit the earth. ... Blessed are the merciful, for they shall obtain mercy" (Matt 5:5, 7).

The world, of course, argues otherwise. We live in a day when aggressive and assertive ways are touted while reticence and deference are ridiculed. Examine the self-improvement section of your bookstore and you find titles like *The Art of Getting Your Own Sweet Way, The Virtue of Selfishness, Competitive Advantage,* and *How To Get What You Want.* These titles seem to suggest that you should get what you want even if you have to use or abuse people. Society too often applauds the coercive, and almost canonizes the ruthless.

---

5. Scripture quotations in this article are from the Revised Standard Version.

Yet on the sundown side of the day, when the applause and cheers are but an echo and the prizes have tarnished, whom does history affirm?

And around the time of Jesus' birth, where would we have looked for the world's hope to be revealed? In the compound of Herod, who called himself "the Great"? In the quarters of Quirinius, Roman legate of Syria? In the palace of Caesar on the Palatine Hill in Rome? Unlike the boastings of Herod, Augustus, and Quirinius, the Word of God was whispered in Jesus. The birth of Jesus was surprising with its inconspicuous setting, its simplicity and reticence. But who made the lasting impression?

On his seventieth birthday, the great medical scientist Louis Pasteur was honored at a jubilee celebration in the amphitheater of the Sorbonne. In his appreciation speech, Pasteur noted that "nations will unite, not to destroy, but to build. ... The future will belong to those who have done most for suffering humanity."

The future does indeed belong to strong but gentle people like William Carey, William and Catherine Booth, Frances Willard, Albert Schweitzer, Dorothy Day, Jean Vanier, Mother Teresa of Calcutta, and Martin Luther King, Jr. In those who say yes to Jesus' presence, a

Christlike spirit is born, which soon issues in human deeds of constancy and quiet strength.

Jesus came as a sign, and still he moves and acts where loving people act in gentle ways from great strength, where people see possibility and respond with skill, kindness, generosity, and courage.

Jesus also came as a lowly sign, and still he comes where people admit their need and limitations, where they sense that whatever power or gifts they may have do not so much reside in them as work through them. Jesus reminded his followers that this response was to be theirs: "Whoever exalts himself will be humbled, and whoever humbles himself will be exalted" (Matt 23:12). He also told the disciples: "You know that those who are supposed to rule over the Gentiles lord it over them, and their great men exercise authority over them. But it shall not be so among you; but whoever would be great among you must be your servant, and whoever would be first among you must be slave of all" (Mark 10:42–44).

In the Sermon on the Mount, Jesus encapsulated this teaching in one of the beatitudes, "Blessed are the poor in spirit" (Matt 5:3), which might be translated, "Blessed are the humble-minded." Jesus also taught that the "first will be last, and the last first" (Matt 19:30).

But today, Jesus' teachings and his spirit are often disdained by a world that treats privilege and position as the authentic measure of greatness and power, that gauges another's worth by the circle of acquaintances he lunches with, by the size of his paycheck, or by the neighborhood he can afford to live in. In an age so particular about rank and status, many people seriously object to serving anyone. (Although those dupes may be more enslaved to their jobs or their images than they realize.)

Or people dismiss Jesus' teachings and his spirit as impractical when it comes to the competitive struggles of business and profession, or politics and international relations. "I've tried to run my business by the Sermon on the Mount, but it doesn't work," some say. It does take struggle and prayer; it may cost something, but it is not impossible. People do it.

Indeed, the world's ways of pride, competition, and status-seeking wound others and leave us empty. The stresses and pressures of staying on the defensive, "getting the biggest bone," and overpowering someone else have contributed to shaky marriages and ugly divorces, heart disease and ulcers, abused children, the arms race, the drug crisis, and a host of other problems that blight our lives.

We need the humble-minded, unpretentious, God-centered life that Jesus lived and to which he summons us. We need him to awaken our hunger for goodness, and move us toward community, responsibility, and reverence for God. We need to be infected with the contagion of inspiration and influence, that rouses us to claim wholeness and a life fit for living, fit for dying, and fit for a destiny beyond both.

God gave us a sign when Jesus took upon himself the humble form of a servant. "Have this mind among yourselves," the apostle Paul wrote, "which is yours in Christ Jesus, who, though he was in the form of God, did not count equality with God a thing to be grasped, but emptied himself, taking the form of a servant, being born in the likeness of men. And being found in human form he humbled himself and became obedient unto death, even death on a cross" (Phil 2:5–8).

The wealth of empire, the strength of conquering armies, the snare of celebrity, the drive to elbow our way to the top—are these the measure of our humanity or the evidence of true power? No, the sign for all times is in a stable where a child is born whose name is Jesus, who took the form of a servant to reveal the love that saves us and keeps us.

✦

A Cosmic Culmination

Charles Colson with Catherine Larson

Sometime this Christmas season, you are sure to hear those rousing words of Handel's *Messiah*, taken from Revelation 11:15: "The kingdom of this world has become the kingdom of our Lord and of his Christ" (ESV). Tradition has it that the music so moved King George II that he stood to his feet out of respect for an even greater King. The rest of the audience followed, as have audiences for generations since. The Hallelujah Chorus is the culmination of our Messiah's story, a story that Handel rightly showed was foretold by the Prophets, heralded in the Annunciation, and has at its heart a message about a king and a kingdom.

Sadly, that kingdom message is often missed in our saccharine retelling of the Christmas story. Somehow we glaze over the angel's words to Mary, that she will give birth to a son whose "kingdom will never end" (Luke 1:33).[6] The myopia continues as we read the Gospels. We skim over pages of kingdom references. We miss Christ's inaugural address when he opens the scroll of Isaiah and proclaims that Scripture has been fulfilled in the people's hearing (Luke 4:21). We muddle through the parables that tell us repeatedly, "The kingdom of God is like ..." And we glance over the very reason our Savior was crucified, a sign crudely scrawled beneath the cross: "Jesus of Nazareth, King of the Jews" (John 19:19).

Along the way, the Good News is truncated. An earth-shaking, kingdom-sized announcement is reduced to a personal self-help story. Our gospel has grown too small.

So what was Jesus talking about when he came announcing a kingdom?

He was talking about the eschatological certainty that in the end, God's reign will be made manifest. His message is teleological; it is to *the world*. It is not just to us

---

6. Unless otherwise noted, Scripture quotations in this article are from the New International Version (1984).

as individuals: "Come to the cross and you can be saved."
As wonderfully significant as that is for every one of us,
and as grateful as I will always be for the night that Christ
came into my life, it's all part of a much larger purpose.
I am being saved from my sin so that I may serve him in
the building of his kingdom, the establishing of his rule.
The really good news is that the gospel isn't just about
you or me. God has saved us as part of a larger plan, the
coming of his kingdom.

It merits mentioning that surveying the Gospels
reveals a dual reality to this kingdom. In one sense, Jesus
brings the kingdom with his coming. He heals the sick
and drives out demons as a way of proclaiming that the
kingdom of God is at hand. And he underscores its present reality when he states, "From the days of John the
Baptist until now, the kingdom of heaven has been force-
fully advancing" (Matt 11:12a). But elsewhere Jesus talks
of the kingdom as a coming reality. When he takes the
cup with his disciples, for instance, he states, "I tell you
the truth, I will not drink again of the fruit of the vine
until that day when I drink it anew in the kingdom of
God" (Mark 14:25). Prominent New Testament scholar
Herman Ridderbos wrote in *The Coming of the Kingdom*
that Jesus proclaims a kingdom "both as a present and as

a future reality." In my book *God and Government*, I discuss this very point. As Augustine taught, while we live in the kingdom of man, we are to live as citizens of the kingdom of God. In some ways it recalls the Allies' triumph in World War II. Jesus' coming is D-day; his second coming will be V-day. The kingdom of God has been inaugurated with his first advent. But the kingdom of God will not be established in its fullness until his second advent. So we wait and pray for that day, hard as that may be.

In the interim, while we personally cannot usher in the kingdom (only God can do that), we can faithfully live as citizens of the kingdom to come. The Beatitudes, for example, give us a pattern of life for that coming kingdom that we can aim to live out now.

This Christmas, remind yourself and others of the significance of the Incarnation: that one day God will usher in the fullness of his kingdom. The kingdom of this world will become the kingdom of our Lord and of his Christ, and he will reign forever and ever. God will bring about that cosmic culmination. And the chorus of hallelujahs will ring not just for a few stanzas at Christmastime but forevermore.

✧

Misreading the Magnificat

It's hard to find hymns that embody Scripture's sharp critique of the rich.

David Neff

When Mary came to visit, Elizabeth's child leaped in her womb. Mary's spirit, too, jumped to a higher plane. In the inspired exchange between the cousins, the pregnant virgin sang a prophetic hymn of praise for God's salvation. In that prophecy, Mary praised God for filling the hungry with good things and sending the rich away empty. We call her hymn the "Magnificat," and we Christians have been singing it as a regular part of worship since about the year 500.

For most of the 1,500 years since, congregations and cloistered monks and nuns chanted the straight, unadorned biblical text of Mary's song. In the latter half of the 20th century, however, musical paraphrases of the Magnificat flourished. One of my favorites is Timothy Dudley-Smith's bold four-square hymn, "Tell Out, My Soul." Others inhabited the folk idiom: Christopher Idle's "My Soul Proclaims the Greatness of the Lord," Rory Cooney's "Canticle of the Turning," and John Michael Talbot's "Holy Is His Name."

As a worship musician who tries to fine-tune what we sing with the Scriptures we read, I have felt frustrated by the way musicians blunt the Magnificat's protest against the 1 percent (to borrow Occupy language). Take Dudley-Smith's otherwise excellent "Tell Out, My Soul" as an example. Five years younger than his Cambridge friend John Stott, Dudley-Smith was part of the circle that renewed English evangelical hymnody midcentury. But in "Tell Out, My Soul," he focused on the first half of Mary's poetic parallelism that contrasted the powerful with the humble and neglected the second half that counterpoised God's treatment of the hungry with the rich. Talbot and Cooney commit the same sin of omission. Idle's text is the refreshing exception.

It is easy to spiritualize power and turn it into pride. Thus Dudley-Smith's rendering: "Proud hearts and stubborn wills are put to flight."

Now, we know that pride and stubbornness are not the exclusive province of the rich. If the Holy Spirit had wanted to talk about these vicious habits of the heart, he would have inspired Mary along those lines only. But he didn't, fingering the rich along with the powerful. As a Church of England bishop, Dudley-Smith may have thought wealth too delicate a matter for his Scripture song.

It is hard to find Christian hymns that embody Scripture's sharp critique of the rich and the dangers of wealth. There are positive songs about simplicity ("Simple Gifts") and exhortations not to cling to earthly goods (the German Lutheran chorales "A Mighty Fortress" and "Jesus, Priceless Treasure"), but not much on the actual dangers of wealth.

Scripture's sharp-edged message about the danger of wealth is not restricted to the Magnificat. One of my favorite gospel songs adapts Jesus' story of the rich man and Lazarus—"Rusty Old Halo" by Hoyt Axton. Unfortunately, Axton of "Joy to the World (Jeremiah

Was a Bullfrog)" fame blunted the parable by reducing the fires of hell to "a rusty old halo, skinny white cloud, robe that's so wooly it scratches."

There's a refreshingly unusual folk ballad on Keith and Kristyn Getty's new album, *Hymns for the Christian Life*. Think of "Simple Living" as the musical equivalent of Shane Claiborne and Tony Campolo's *Red Letter Revolution*. Unlike Axton's soft-pedaling, the Getty-Stuart Townend songwriting team gives Jesus' dialogue with the rich young ruler a transparent treatment. They hone the sharp edge of Jesus' advice: "Sell all you have; give to the poor. / Then heaven's treasure shall be yours." Francis of Assisi couldn't have said it more pointedly.

The last lines of the song's first verse are also close to Jesus' original: "How hard for those who are rich on earth / To gain the wealth of heaven." The second verse focuses on the widow's mite story. It concludes, "Not what you give but what you keep / Is what the King is counting." Keith recently told me that with this album he wanted to join worship to everyday life. Thus it addresses work, suffering, community, family, doubt—and money. "A more quotidian approach to theology," he calls it. Props to the Gettys and Townend for giving us lyrics that present Jesus' message unbated.

I don't want to argue here about what Jesus meant in his criticism of mammon and his threats toward the rich. That's a debate for a different space. But however you interpret those statements, they are harsh and wounding. Keith says that he wants to make us traditionalists uncomfortable with songs like this.

Those who paraphrase Scripture have a special duty to let it speak with its proper force. Add a good tune, and you've fortified those words to shape our lives.

✡

Let the Pagans Have the Holiday

Rodney Clapp

I t is time to recognize that a new tradition has been added to Christmas. As surely as trees and lights and reindeer, December now brings Christian complaints about the secularization of the holiday. T-shirts and posters and preachers declare, "Jesus Is the Reason for the Season," but their protests are drowned in the commercial deluge.

Christmas is ruled not from Jerusalem or Rome or Wheaton or any other religious center, but from Madison Avenue and Wall Street. In a revealing symbolic act, President George Bush two years ago inaugurated the season not, mind you, in a church, but in a shopping mall. There he bought some socks and reminded Americans their true Christmas responsibility is not veneration but consumption.

To some, Christmas also seems less Christian because many of the nation's institutions are less and less willing to prop up the church. So some disgruntled believers—misguidedly, by my estimate—do battle with various courthouses that no longer allow creches on their lawns.

Sometimes outsiders glimpse our own dilemma more acutely than we can. Last Christmas, Rabbi Lawrence Hoffman wrote an article in Cross Currents entitled, "Being a Jew at Christmas Time." In it he observed, "There is nothing wrong with sleigh bells, Bing Crosby, and Christmas pudding, but I should hope Christians would want more than just that, and as Christmas becomes more and more secularized, I am not sure they get it." He went on: "In the end, the problem of Christmas is not mine any more than Christmas itself is. The real Christmas challenge belongs to Christians: how to take Christmas out of the secularized public domain and move it back into the religious sphere once again."

The rabbi is right on both counts. For Christians, Christmas definitely loses something—in fact, loses its core—as it gets more and more secular. But the solution is not to worry over courthouse creches: The real Christmas challenge belongs to Christians. The church and not city hall is charged with witnessing to the gospel and remembering to the world the birth of Jesus Christ.

Here I want to suggest that Christians may best reclaim Christmas, indirectly, by first reclaiming Easter. Ours is an ironic faith, one that trains its adherents to see strength in weakness. The irony at hand could be that a secularizing culture has shown us something important by devaluing Christmas. In a way, Christians have valued Christmas too much and in the wrong way. I defer again to Hoffman, who writes,

> Historians tell us that Christmas was not always the cultural fulcrum that balances Christian life. There was a time when Christians knew that the paschal mystery of death and resurrection was the center of Christian faith. It was Easter that really mattered, not Christmas. Only in the consumer-conscious nineteenth century did Christmas overtake Easter, becoming the centerpiece of popular piety. Madison Avenue marketed

the change, and then colluded with the entertainment industry to boost Christmas to its current calendrical prominence.

The Bible, of course, knows nothing of the designated holidays we call Easter or Christmas. But each holiday celebrates particular events, and there can be no doubt which set of events receives the most scriptural emphasis.

It is well known that all four Gospels build toward and focus on the events leading up to and including what we commemorate at Easter. One-quarter to one-half the chapters in each of the four Gospels deal with Easter events. Clearly, the gospel traditions see these as the crucial episodes, the events that identify and ratify Jesus as God's Messiah. In fact, two of the four Gospels (Mark and John) have no birth, or Christmas, narratives. This means certain of the earliest Christian communities knew no Christmas (at least, not from their basic texts). To put it another way, we could be Christians without the stories of Christmas, but not without the stories of Easter.

The rest of the New Testament does not deviate from this pattern. The earliest recorded Christian sermon (in Acts 2) proclaims the Easter message of the world's Savior crucified and then raised by Israel's God. And what can we say of Paul, who nowhere speaks of Jesus' birth, but everywhere heralds "Jesus Christ and him crucified" (1 Cor 2:2) and warns that "if Christ has not been raised, then our preaching is in vain and your faith is in vain" (15:14 RSV)?

To this day, Christian worship is marked by Easter more than by Christmas. Consider the sacraments (or ordinances, if you prefer). Baptism is baptism into Christ's crucifixion and resurrection. As Paul writes, "We have been buried with him by baptism into death, so that, just as Christ was raised from the dead by the glory of the Father, so we too might walk in newness of life" (Rom 6:4, NRSV). Celebrating the Eucharist, or Communion, includes rich themes drawing both from Christ's passion and his resurrection. And of course, we gather to worship on the day of the Lord's rising, so that Christians for centuries have thought of each Sunday as a "little Easter."

The recovery of Easter as our pivotal holy day may best be served by a recovery of the Christian calendar, complete with the cycle of seasons that recall the gospel from Advent to Christmas to Epiphany to Lent to Easter and Pentecost. The calendar, like the gospel narrative, builds toward and pivots around the focal events of Christ's passion and Easter. Recognizing the liturgical year is a large step toward seeing Easter as the main Christian holiday.

In calling Christians to return to the Christian calendar and return Easter to its rightful prominence, I am not implying that the events of Christmas are trivial or untrue. The nativity stories help us to remember key and glorious truths, such as the Incarnation. But surely Easter, and not the Christmas on which we modern Western Christians focus most of our attention, is the "fulcrum that balances Christian life."

Christmas celebrated without the events of Easter overshadowing is too easily sentimentalized and secularized. A baby in a manger, angels hovering overhead, cattle lowing nearby—surely this idyllic world needs no redemption. A dechristianized Christmas is the ultimate Pelagian holiday; for at what other time of the year can we seem so certain that, merely with good feelings and good will, humanity can save itself? Annually, in fact, newspaper editorials and television commentators say exactly that, pleading that all the world needs is to spread Christmas cheer through the year.

But Easter—Easter is on the other side of a cross with nails, of confrontation and beatings and death, and then, only then, resurrection and new life. Christmas we can too easily teach to our kids (and ourselves) without blinking, free of strain or discomfort (provided we gloss, as we usually do, such details as Herod's slaughter of the innocents). Easter is harder, for it requires facing death, the shortcomings of the disciples, the bloody lengths God must go to in order to rescue a confused, hateful world from itself.

All of this is to say we have worried about Christmas too much. Christians in an indifferent and even hostile society need to learn cultural *jujitsu*—to sometimes let the culture push at points where it wants to, and there collapse of its own momentum. This is especially important in our cultural situation, where resistance is so easily itself turned into a marketable commodity. T-shirts and bumper stickers proclaiming "Jesus Is the Reason for the Season" make the message itself into a consumer item.

So let the pagans have Christmas *as their most significant holiday.* Easter is the central *Christian* holiday. And when we are known for our Easter, then we will have our Christmas back.

✧

God's Gift on God's Tree

Ruth Bell Graham

As our children grow and mature, our greatest joy, perhaps, is leading them to realize that the Babe of Bethlehem is in reality the Christ of Calvary.

We have always held precious the familiar childhood memories of Christmas, the sparkling tree with all its decorations, the excitement of secrets and surreptitious hiding of gifts. But Christmas to us is far more than these things, and is of infinitely deeper significance than seasonal excitement. And we believe that children who are blessed with Christian homes and listen to the Christmas story and the happy carols can, even at a very early age, learn something of the spiritual significance of it all, namely, a Gift and a Tree that give Christmas its meaning.

As Christmas approaches once more, we Christian parents long that our children experience both the fun we knew as children and at the same time the reality of the Christ Child as Savior and Lord in their lives.

Many years ago something of the true meaning of Christmas dawned upon me as I realized for the first time that the precious baby for whom there was no place at the inn was in truth the eternal Son of God, the Creator of the world. In his Incarnation I came to see that he was but entering the world he had created himself, coming from the living heart of the Father to redeem the people of his own creation.

Now as I have experienced the miracle of bringing precious lives into the world, I am, as a Christian mother, faced with the responsibility as well as the privilege of leading these little hearts to know Christ without whom life is empty and through whom life is abundant and eternal.

All of us are in this world as a result of physical birth; some of us are going to spend an eternity with Christ by reason of spiritual birth. I know little of the shades and implications of theology; but of this I am sure, that at Christmas we shall be celebrating not merely an historical event of two thousand years ago, but a glorious, momentous step in the plan of God's redemption for sinful man, which culminated at the Cross.

This is the reason we want our children to understand what Christmas means. We want them to enjoy the pleasures of a festive holiday season, but far more do we desire that they grasp, even now, as best they can, the knowledge of him who is Emmanuel, "God with us," Savior and Lord. The job is too big for us, we know. But we are aware that "He that spared not his own Son but delivered him up for us all, how shall he not with him freely give us all things?" namely, the wisdom that we need, the understanding and love and grace.

As we pray for our children and think of the things that this world may have in store for them, we know of no better time than Christmas to acknowledge, "For I know whom I have believed, and am persuaded that he is able to keep that which I have committed unto him against that day" (KJV).

And we can claim the assurance: "For the promise is to you and to your children." We have committed them to God and our faith rests implicitly upon his sufficiency.

✧

Christmas Unplugged

Bill McKibben

I'm looking forward to Christmas—no dread of the busyness, no fear of drowning in the commercialism. I know what Christmas Eve will be like: we'll cut the tree in the afternoon and bring it in and decorate it. We'll go to church, where I will sweat with my Sunday-school class as they try to remember their lines for the pageant, and then I'll relax in the knowledge that it is the small mistakes (the drooping halo, the three-year-old shepherd using his crook as a hockey stick) that really stick most fondly in people's minds. We'll come home, read the Christmas story once more, put up our stockings, and go to bed. In the morning, we'll open the stockings and find the candies and pencils and tiny jokes inside; we'll exchange one or two homemade presents—photo albums, raspberry jam made in the summer's heat—and then we'll go outside to play in the snow, or into the kitchen, cooking for the great dinner ahead. In other words, a completely normal Christmas minus the mounds of presents.

The story of how my family arrived at this quiet and beloved Christmas (which means, of course, a much quieter December than most of our friends experience, without a single trip to the mall, and a January without a credit-card debt) has to do with many things: with carbon dioxide levels in the atmosphere, with our worries about what a consumer culture meant for our daughter—and with the conviction, nurtured by our church, that there was more real joy to be had from Christmas if only we could unplug it: more real connections with that glad day in the past, and more real hope for a troubled future.

Consumption is an issue uniquely suited for faith communities. Among the institutions of our society, only the church and the synagogue and the mosque can still posit some reason for human existence *other* than the constant accumulation of stuff. Our businesses thrive on constant growth; our politicians avoid hard choices by flogging the economy to grow more quickly (in the immortal words of William Jefferson Clinton, "It's the economy, stupid"); even our educational institutions have designed themselves to fit easily into this happy picture. We have made most important decisions—as individuals and as a nation—in recent decades by answering the question: Is it good for the economy?

Religious institutions, which grew up before this emphasis, inherited a different set of concerns—in many ways, a contradictory set of concerns—and those contradictions, among other things, have weakened the power of religion in the economic era. We profess to believe that we cannot worship both God and mammon; we profess to worship someone who told us to give away, not accumulate; we profess to follow a tradition that in its earliest and purest forms demanded communal sharing of goods and money. But we have by and large bracketed off those central portions of the message. And we are not alone in this. Virtually every religious and philosophic tradition has similar figures and similar teachings, in a line that runs from Buddha through Jesus and Francis, to Thoreau and Gandhi. Martin Luther King, Jr., said at the end of his life that it was not racism or imperialism or militarism that represented our root problem, it was materialism. But for all our pious lip service, we have regarded those people as unrealistic cranks.

This is a powerful moment for rehabilitating Christ the crank. What are the atmospheric chemists telling us? What are the climatologists saying? In many ways, the same things we have heard from Christ and his disciples: Simplicity, they say. Community. Not because it is good for our souls, or for our right relation with God, but because without simpler lives, the chances of stabilizing the planet's basic workings are slim. Because without community, the chances for buses and trains and other necessary efficiencies are nil. This confluence of the hardheaded and the softhearted may make for a powerful moment, an unpredictable time when the world could turn quickly in new directions.

If we in religious communities are going to do anything about it, we have to recognize just how strong the consumerist ethos is. It has taken root in all of us, basically unchallenged. Fertilized by a million commercials, it has grown into what we call a wolf tree where I live, a tree whose canopy spreads so wide that it blots out the sun, that it blots out the quiet word of God. Churches, obviously, do not have the power to compete head-on, and few of us junkies are ready to go cold turkey. But increasingly there are signs that people are asking deep questions: "Isn't there something more than this?" And the churches can help build this momentum in important ways, beginning with those things it has the most psychological control over.

Chief on this list is the celebration of Christmas, not only the most beloved of church holidays, but also the most powerful celebration of consumerism. Just how powerful can be judged from the fact that it has become a major gift-giving holiday in Japan, despite the conspicuous lack of Christians there. And it is not entirely well-understood. A few years ago, in Kyoto, one department store filled its center window with an enormous effigy of a crucified Santa Claus.

Christmas is a school for consumerism—in it we learn to equate delight with materialism. We celebrate the birth of One who told us to give everything to the poor by giving each other motorized tie racks.

A few years ago, with a couple of friends, I launched a campaign in our Methodist conference in the Northeast for "Hundred Dollar Holidays," recommending that families try to spend no more than a hundred dollars on Christmas.

When we began, we were very long faced, talking a lot about the environmental damage that Christmas caused (all those batteries!), and the money that could instead go to social justice work, and so on. But what we found was that this did not do the trick, either for us or for our fellow congregants.

What did the trick, we discovered, was focusing on *happier* holidays. Though we continued to stress the $100 figure as an anchor for families pushed and pulled by the tidal forces of advertising and social expectation, we talked about making Christmas more fun. The poster we used suggests many alternatives to a store-bought Christmas, things that involve people doing things for each other and for creation.

We were amazed at how well this worked, even on the limited scale on which we were trying it out—many people thanked us for "giving them permission" to celebrate Christmas "the way I always wanted to celebrate it." It taught me a useful lesson: that the effect of consumerism on the planet is mirrored precisely in its effect on the soul; that finding true joy means passing up momentary pleasure; and that joy, that deep bubbling joy, is the only really subversive force left in our society. The only way to make people doubt, even for a minute, the inevitability of their course in life is to show them they are being cheated of the truest happiness. And Christmas is a good school for this education, because it can be such a wonderfully giddy party for the birth of a baby.

These questions about consumption, like the questions about the new environmental damage, get near the deepest theological questions. If we were built, then what were we built for? We know what hawks were built for—it's announced in every fiber of their bodies. But what about us? Why do we have this amazing collection of sinews, senses, and sensibilities? Were we really designed to recline on the couch, extending our wrists perpendicular to the floor so we can flick through the television's offerings? Were we really designed in order to shop some more so the economy can grow some more? Or were we designed to experience the great epiphanies that come from contact with each other and with the natural world? Were we designed to witness the goodness all around us, and to protect and nourish it? Just as "the environment" is a context, not an issue, so is "consumption." It defines at the moment who we are—and who we aren't.

This is a profound moment for religious people. On the one hand, our species asserts itself as never before. We have grown large enough to alter creation—whether by the single great explosion of a nuclear weapon, or the billion muffled explosions of pistons inside engines spewing out carbon dioxide. As Oppenheimer said on that New Mexico afternoon testing of the A-bomb, we have become as gods. And not just the nuclear engineers—anyone with a car, anyone with a credit card.

Yet, at the same moment, we have acquired the intelligence to see what we are doing—not just the scientific understanding of things like the greenhouse effect, but the dawning ecological understanding of the way that everything is linked to everything else, that creation is a fabric far richer than any of our predecessors could have understood (though, of course, they may have sensed it more deeply than we do). The age-old struggle between God and mammon, always before a personal and never-ending battle, now has a time limit and a bottom line.

It is really an issue of who or what we put at the center of our lives. In the environmental debates, there has been a lot of discussion about anthropocentrism versus biocentrism versus theocentrism. Most of this debate seems empty to me, assuming as it does that most of us put any of these things at the center. If we followed any of them in a sincere fashion, we would be well on the way to solving our environmental and social problems. Anthropocentrism, if we really placed humans at the center of our concern, would lead inevitably to the kind of sharing necessary to heal the environmentally destructive gaps between rich and poor; were we truly anthropocentric, we would feel grave shame at our own overconsumption. But, of course, we are not. We are me-centric. We are I-dolatrous. That is what consumer society has schooled us to be.

The question now is, how can we break out of it? Some have criticized secular environmentalists as "pagans" because they profess a biocentrism, a view of the world that puts all living things at its center. But they are far closer to orthodoxy than most of the rest of us who still put ourselves at the sweet center. We need to put God there. And then we need to realize that this involves more than the smug announcement that we have done so.

Having God at the center imposes certain limits on our behavior. If we are not to wreck God's creation, then there are certain things we simply must not do; we simply must not continue consuming as we now are. And there are certain things we must do; we must share our bounty with those of the rest of the world, finding somewhere a middle ground so they don't follow our path to consumer development. These things are in one way extraordinarily difficult. But we know the deep and certain joy they can bring, and so we can say with some confidence that at least they are possible. At least they are worth a try.

And we will know if we are succeeding by the evidence all around us. Creation will let us know if we are rebuilding our house, restoring its foundations. Are species continuing to die out? Is the temperature continuing to climb? Our communities will show us if we are really changing. Are the numbers of absurdly rich and absurdly poor beginning to decline? Are we rebuilding institutions other than the mall, places like schools and parks and churches? The environmental crisis is so deep and so fundamental that our response will reveal who we most truly are.

In the meantime, I'm looking forward to Christmas. There's one more tradition we always observe, one begun many centuries ago by Saint Francis. We take some bird seed out into the woods near our homes, and spread it far and wide. The minute we leave I have no doubt that jays and squirrels and chickadees and shrews descend, happy to have their day's food without a day's work. This is such a joyful morning that all creation deserves to share in the celebration!

✧

The Prince of Peace

Addison H. Leitch

A little verse by Mary Coleridge keeps running through my mind. It begins with a pretty Christmas picture and ends with a kind of threat: "I saw a stable, low and very bare / A little child in a manger. ... The safety of the world was lying there / And the world's danger." The poem begins with all the happy memories of a child's Christmas and progresses, as we progress in our later years, to another kind of understanding.

I find myself a little suspicious of those who write autobiographies that are perfectly clear and specific about what they experienced and what they understood in their childhood. My memories are not so sound, and with the best of will and the hardest effect at remembering I end up with many blanks; but I usually do gather some over-all impressions out of the confused and usually rosy glow. Christmas, for example, was always a good thing, but a confused thing: fireplaces and candy canes, Christmas entertainments and those awful church goodies (pure delights then), whisperings and surprises. There was the morning of the bicycle, and that time I awoke early in the morning to go down for a first peek only to discover that my dad was just on his way to bed. Later came that awful day when a bunch of us were seated on the front steps of somebody's house, doing whatever youngsters do on front steps, clustered about with tricycles, balls, dolls, sticks, and cookies, and little Josephine Hunter (how her name sticks in my mind) told me there was no Santa Claus. I dashed home to get the straight story from my mother, who had some kind of lame excuse about the spirit of Santa Claus and the spirit of Christmas and the Spirit of God and his great gift of Jesus, which had to do with all the Christmas gifts. It simply wouldn't do then, but it worked out better later. Under the tree we had a train mixed up with a crèche and some sheep on a hill-side behind the railroad station, and a series of doodads that broke up before Christmas dinner, but a Christmas dinner that was good for food and a delight to the eyes. Then there was the day that girl from our second grade caught fire in her flannelette nightgown on Christmas morning and the Christmas day a wounded soldier was a visitor in our home. You took the bad with the good, but it was mostly good.

The big change in Christmas comes when you begin to notice that most of your Christmas gifts have become "useful" instead of fun. (Of course, money was always both useful and fun.) Then comes the biggest change of all: your own children appear on the scene, and you begin to give instead of get. That becomes the best of all. Somehow in your anxiety to give and make happy in the giving there is a great insight into a loving Father, who loves us with an everlasting love and would shower gifts on us continually and surely must want us to be happy and grateful. One can continue to grow up into an appreciation of all that.

But other things come to mind. The Christmas-card picture of Christmas always has shadows in the background. There were no halos there, and maybe the manger was cold and dirty. One thing we are sure of is that Herod used this homey occasion for his slaughter of the innocents: all kinds of babies were killed and mothers pierced to the heart. The flight to Egypt makes a nice picture, with the little burro and all, but it was a flight in fear. The return to Nazareth was under the threat of continued cruelty in those cruel days, and as the boy Jesus grew up in that little country town his mother's heart was often pierced—long before the cross—as she pondered his destiny. The baby was called Jesus (Joshua, Jason—Savior) because he would save his people from their sins, but he could do it only along the Via Dolorosa, and they nailed his fine, pure body to a tree, and his mother was there. It is all a strange, strange story, but men have come to see that it is THE story; it is the plot of history, the meaning of things for the whole of the cosmos.

This one whose birth meant that many others would have to die for him, this one who promised wars and rumors of wars, this one who died in agony between two thieves, who brought out the best in men and also their worst—this one was called the Prince of Peace. It is a strange title for such a one, for one who lived and died as he did, who set so many desperate currents loose in history. Did something go wrong somewhere or have we read it all wrong?

The Prince of Peace: "The safety of the world was lying there / And the world's danger." Our trouble is that we want the Peace without the Prince. Neither men nor nations will have him rule over them, and that is the world's danger, because that one who called himself the Way did not allow for any other way and we refuse to follow that Way. From the garden of Eden to the gardens of upper suburbia it is still a question of obedience: we will not obey and so we are shut out of Paradise. It is not that God would keep Paradise from us—he longs for us to have it as any loving Father would; but he cannot give it to us apart from the only Way in which Paradise is possible. We are fighting against God and so fighting against our highest felicity (in his will is our peace), and it is not that God will not but that he cannot. Our disobedience is not only against the basic essence of our beings, our creaturehood, our dependence and contingence, but against the structure of everything, against the stars in their courses, against the way things are, really are. As H. H. Farmer once said, "If you go against the grain of the universe you will get splinters."

A friend of mine who likes to twit me about my religion delights in throwing up the condition of the world today after two thousand years of the Prince of Peace. I am shut up to only one defense. We cannot have the Peace without the Prince, and we still refuse to have him.

The Bible is clear: "Of the increase of his government and peace there shall be no end," but we still want his peace without his government. Note how Paul speaks of the armor of the Christian and how specifically and directly one may have the helmet and the shield and the sword, but when it comes to peace he speaks of our feet being "shod with the preparation of the *gospel* of peace." And there are the "things that *make* for peace."

Peace is likely the prayer of every sensitive heart in these awful days, but the hope of peace seems farther and farther away as larger and larger combinations of power challenge one another with greater and greater engines of destruction. If only they would not "learn war any more," if Africa or Palestine or Russia or China would only settle down, maybe then we could have some peace. But "from whence come wars and fightings among us? Come they not hence, even of our lusts that war in our members?" Would a multiplication of my own heart to the hearts of all men bring peace or war? Where does the problem lie? Am I myself a center of peace or of discord? How quickly do I flare up and over what inanities? What bitterness do I nurse, what resentments do I harbor? It all moves out from men to nations: we cry peace and there is no peace.

The Great Commission seems such an old and ordinary program in the midst of all the other programs clamoring for attention, all the utopias. World missions seems a weak and ineffective kind of effort over against atomic power and space flight, and in human terms it is. So was a babe in a manger and a boy in Nazareth, and a poor rabbi on a cross. But the foolishness of God is wiser, the weakness of God is stronger. If you can believe that, you will still hold on to that kind of Prince with that kind of Way until the Peace comes. If you cannot so believe, the available options seem to have pretty well run out.

✧

Peace: At Times a Sword and Fire

Billy Graham

Over and over we hear quoted the message of the angels to the shepherds, "Glory to God in the highest, and on earth peace, good will toward men" (Luke 2:14 KJV). Yet even in Scripture there are two rarely quoted statements by Jesus that seem to contradict the message of the angels. How can we reconcile that message with Luke 12:49, where Jesus said, "I have come to bring fire on the earth" (NIV), or with Matthew 10:34, where he said, "Do not suppose that I have come to bring peace to the earth. I did not come to bring peace, but a sword. For I have come to turn a man against his ... [family]—and a man's enemies will be the members of his own household" (NIV). These two statements seem to contradict the announcement of the angels on that first Christmas.

Probably thousands of people in Christ's day did not understand when he said he would set fire to the earth. There were good-hearted, kind people anxious for a better world. Idealistic, they were ignorant of the deep-seated disease of human nature, and looked at the world through rose-tinted glasses. They were like the mother of Lee Harvey Oswald, who said, "He was always such a good boy." They were like the professors of Heidelberg University who praised the character of Joseph Goebbels when he was getting his PhD degree. They were like the people of Buenos Aires who thought Adolph Eichmann was a model citizen. They were like the people described in the book *While England Slept*—they could see a crisis, but could not believe it was so deep.

Many people do not know the deep-seated evil within human nature. They do not know how deeply fixed are the roots of pride, greed, selfishness, and lust in human society. They cannot believe that Jeremiah was right when he said, "The heart is deceitful above all things and beyond cure" (Jer 17:9 NIV). They cannot believe that the result of sin is spiritual death, and that a holy God judges sin in nations as well as individuals. Their understanding of evil in the world is superficial. It may seem to them that everything can easily be put right by better understanding between peoples, by better education, and by social solutions.

That first Christmas night when the announcement to the shepherds was made, it might have seemed to indicate that the optimists were right when the angels said, "Glory to God in the highest, and on earth peace, good will toward men." However, such optimists had ignored Isaiah 53, which declared that the Coming Servant would be despised and rejected by men. They had ignored the prophecies that the world would rebel against him. They could believe Jesus was the Messiah, but not that he would have to die—and die on a cross.

Today many well-meaning people, relying on a superficial knowledge of the Bible, are making this mistake. Jesus had to correct such easy optimism and warn people that his coming does not mean a quick utopia. He had to make clear to them that his coming, far from meaning peace, means spiritual warfare. Far from being a drug to soothe society to sleep—with man's evil nature still smoldering and liable to explode at any moment—his message is a fire that will set society ablaze with moral choices, bringing divisions even in families. William Barclay commented on Matthew 10, "When some great cause emerges, it is bound to divide people; there are bound to be those who answer and those who refuse the challenge.

"To be confronted with Jesus is necessarily to be confronted with the choice whether to accept him or to reject him; and the world is always divided into those who have accepted Christ and those who have not. The bitterest thing about this warfare was that a man's foes would often be those of his own household." Those who are dominated by selfishness, lust, and prejudice will fight the change that Christ wants to bring to their lives, to their family, and to their world. Thus, there will be division and strife. This is a fundamental truth not only of the Bible but of the conditions round about us this Christmas. We will only delude ourselves if we try to be more optimistic than Christ.

The basic problem facing our world is not just social inequity, lack of education, or even physical hunger. We are finding that highly educated and well-fed people have greed, hate, passion, and lust that are not eliminated by any known process of education. The roots of sin in our hearts are extremely deep, and this is the basic cause of the world's problems. Only the fire of the Lord can burn those roots out.

This is precisely what Christ came to do. He did not come to treat symptoms, he came to get at the heart of man's disease. That is what Good Friday and Easter are all about.

Christ's own statements about fire and the sword are probably a shock to many who have missed them. I do not think I have ever heard a sermon on them. We have been taught that Jesus was the Prince of Peace, and indeed he was. We have been taught that he was the very incarnation of the everlasting love, and he was. But we have misunderstood the divine definition of peace, and we have misunderstood the divine definition of love.

How can this loving, peaceful Christ be reconciled with the flame-setting, sword-bearing Christ? There is no contradiction at all. John Wesley interpreted Christ's statement as meaning, "I come to spread the fire of heavenly love over all the earth."

In a sense, true love is a fire. It can never be complacent. The Bible speaks of it as a "refiner's fire." The man who loves his school most shouts the loudest for his team at a football game. The man who loves his country most will fight to preserve its freedom. The man who loves his neighbor most will fight against all that hurts, deprives, and oppresses his neighbor. "Who is led into sin," shouted Paul the apostle, "and I do not inwardly burn?" (2 Cor 11:29 NIV).

Think how Christ, with righteous indignation, criticized the Pharisees for plundering widows' houses, rebuked those who wanted to stone a helpless adulterous woman, and drove the moneychangers out of the temple. Those who love our country will likewise do everything they can to work for social justice, law and order, and world peace.

Jesus warned that when we take sides against evil we will be opposed by those who do not understand the deep problem of human nature and a true definition of love.

When Abraham Lincoln was 22 years old, he visited New Orleans and saw a slave girl being pinched, prodded, and trotted up and down the room like a horse to show what good merchandise she was. Lincoln was deeply affected. It was on this trip that he formed his opinion of slavery. It ran its searing iron into him then and there. Lincoln touched the arm of his companion and said tensely, "Boys, let's get away from this. If I ever get a chance to hit that thing, I'll hit it hard." Lincoln loved people deeply, whatever their color. And because he loved them, his soul blazed against the slave trade with an intense and relentless hatred. He fought against it with a passion that finally burned it out of existence.

However, Lincoln's love for men did not bring peace and unity. It did not bring him a high popularity rating. Rather, as his biographies show, it created strife and division. It took a war, a bloodbath, to wash away this tyranny. He was criticized more than any president in American history, and his stand eventually cost him his life. However, it brought him the inward peace of conscience that a man can know only when he is morally right. Ultimately it brought him the admiration of the world and made a place for him in history almost unparalleled by any other American.

Like Lincoln, Winston Churchill was faced with severe opposition. No man loved England more, but during the 1930s he was mercilessly criticized when he warned about the growing power and ambition of Hitler.

In the same way, the love of God will force us to take sides when we are confronted with moral evil. If we love the poor and underprivileged, we will want to destroy the slums and ghettos, which have no place in affluent America. If we love the young people of America, we will do everything in our power to destroy things that hurt their character and jeopardize their future, things such as drugs and pornography.

L ove is never neutral. To preserve some things, it must destroy others. And that will inevitably stir opposition. So Jesus taught that love for God or love for neighbor (or love for country) does not necessarily bring peace.

And the love God has for us is ten thousand times more intense than any human love. The Bible says, "God so loved the world that he gave his only begotten Son." He came to burn out of the hearts of men and out of society the lust, greed, selfishness, and other evils rooted there. Yet he was despised and rejected—crucified! The blackest picture of the human heart portrays the cross, where evil Roman soldiers murdered him.

But they could not destroy the flame of his love. The Bible teaches that he rose again; this Christ is in the world today with his sword and his fire, fighting against all forms of evil: lust, selfishness, jealousy, hate, oppression. As we approach Christmas 1982, we have a tremendous responsibility to study the issues involved in this matter of peace. Jesus said, "Blessed are the peacemakers."

In pondering peace today, we have something new in history to contend with. Technology has created the most devastating weapons man has ever imagined. To find anything comparable to what we are now facing, one has to turn to the third chapter of 2 Peter, or to the Book of Revelation.

It is possible for man to destroy the planet within a matter of hours. I am not a pacifist, nor am I for unilateral disarmament. But I am for peace, especially when I think of the holocaust approaching. It could blaze upon us at any moment. And weapons of mass destruction that are on the drawing boards—and some even in existence— may be worse than the hydrogen bomb.

I have been calling for SALT X—an agreement among the nations to destroy all weapons of mass destruction. But even while I call for it, I know such an agreement is not likely. Why? Because of the human heart. James asked the question, "What causes fights and quarrels among you? Don't they come from your desires that battle within you?" The technology and the bombs are not the problem. The problem is the heart of man.

Pope John Paul II has said, "Our future on this planet, exposed as it is to nuclear annihilation, depends on one single factor: humanity must make a *moral* about-face."

I am praying that we will recover our moral courage in America. If God grants this, it will light a spiritual fire that must sweep the country. So we must, this Christmas, come to the cross and rededicate ourselves to Jesus Christ, who brought peace—and a sword.

Hallelujah!

Philip Yancey

Just before Christmas of 1988 my wife and I visited London. As the plane banked sharply over the city's center, we saw rowing crews on the Thames, and also Parliament, Whitehall Palace, and other landmark buildings lit in sepia by the slanting rays of morning sun. A fingernail moon hung low in the sky, and the morning star still shone. This was one of London's rare, perfect winter days.

Later that day, half-drunk on coffee, we were dragging along city streets, trying to wrench our biological clocks forward seven time zones by staying awake until dusk. Just before turning in, we lined up in a queue to order some theater tickets. That's when I saw the poster: "One Night Only. Handel's *Messiah* performed by the National Westminster Choir and National Chamber Orchestra at the Barbican Centre." The ticket seller assured me that of all *Messiah* performances in London, this was clearly the best. There were only two problems: the concert would begin in one hour, and it was sold out.

Twenty minutes later, following some spirited intra-marital negotiations, we were in our hotel room squeezing out yet another round of Visine and dressing for a sold-out concert. This moment of serendipity we could not let pass. "Our presence is divinely ordained," I assured my wife. "We are in Handel's home town, where he wrote the piece." Surely a trifling matter like a sellout would not deter us from finding a way inside where we would enjoy an unsurpassed musical experience. Janet's arched eyebrow conveyed unmistakably what she thought of my circumstantial theology, but she indulged me.

After a pell-mell taxi ride to the concert hall, we stumbled across a civic-minded English chap who offered us his extra tickets at half price. My theology was looking better all the time. I started to relax, anticipating a soothing evening of baroque music. Seated on the back row of the main floor, we were ideally positioned for a catnap should the need arise.

I hardly anticipated what I got that evening. I had, of course, heard Handel's *Messiah* often. But something about this time—my sleep-starved, caffeine-buzzed state, the London setting, the performance itself—transported me back closer, much closer, to Handel's day. The event became not just a performance but a kind of epiphany, a striking revelation of Christian theology. I felt able to see beyond the music to the soul of the piece.

As I leaned back in the Barbican Centre's padded seat and listened to the familiar beginning of *Messiah*, it was easy to understand how the oratorio came to be associated with the Advent season. Handel begins with a collection of lilting prophecies from Isaiah about a coming king who will bring peace and comfort to a disturbed and violent world. The music builds, swelling from a solo tenor ("Comfort ye my people ...") to a full chorus joyously celebrating the day when "the glory of the Lord shall be revealed."

I had spent the morning viewing England's remnants of glory, and it occurred to me that just such images of wealth and power must have filled the minds of Isaiah's contemporaries who first heard that promise. I had seen the crown jewels, a solid-gold ruler's mace, and the gilded carriage of the Lord Mayor of London. When the Hebrews heard Isaiah's words, undoubtedly those dispossessed and landless refugees thought back with sharp nostalgia to the glory days of Solomon, when the palace and temple gleamed bright.

Yet rulers who bring a nation glory and prestige often do so by oppressing their subjects and leaching away their wealth. How many poor laborers paid taxes to gild the Lord Mayor's carriage, or King Solomon's residence? Because strong rulers thrive in a climate of fear, even the long-awaited Messiah inspired fear in the prophets. After its boisterous opening, I was surprised to hear Handel's *Messiah* shift so quickly to a somber, even foreboding tone, as if in recognition of this darker side of rulership. The bass warns of a Lord of Hosts who will shake the heavens and the earth, the sea and the dry land.

Israelites were raised with a fear of God so profound that they would not speak or write his name, and from the Messiah they feared not the tyranny of injustice, but rather the prospect of holy justice. "But who may abide the day of his coming?" the contralto cries out in alarm, "For he is like a refiner's fire." If the Lord of Hosts paid a personal visit to corrupted Earth, would any of its inhabitants survive? Would Earth itself survive? The good news of hope hangs in limbo for a moment.

Then out of the tension in Handel's music there soon emerge gentle, familiar words that strikingly resolve the contradiction of a powerful, but comforting ruler: "Behold, a virgin shall conceive, and bear a son, and shall call his name Emmanuel, 'God with us.' " The God who comes to Earth comes not in a raging whirlwind, nor in a devouring fire. He comes instead in the tiniest form imaginable: as an ovum, and then fetus, growing cell by cell inside a humble teenage virgin. In Jesus, God found at last a mode of approach that human beings need not fear: a helpless baby suckling at his mother's breast.

"Behold your God!" the chorus joins in, as if astonished. I wondered how many of the Londoners celebrating Christmas caught the sense of scandal. Stores outside displayed Dickensian scenes of Christmas mirth, and mangers dotted the town squares. But how many grasped the awesome implications of "Immensity cloister'd in thy dear womb"? As G. K. Chesterton once marveled, "The hands that had made the sun and stars were too small to reach the huge heads of the cattle."

Messiah lapses into an orchestral interlude, as if to let listeners ponder the two-pronged mission of a Messiah sent from Almighty God. And then it leaps ahead in time, from the prophets' promises to the stirring birth announcement in a pasture bordering Bethlehem. There, angels proclaimed to quaking shepherds that the reign of fear had ended. Fear not! That very night, God was doing an entirely new thing on Earth: he was becoming one of us. "Glory to God in the highest!" Handel's chorus sings.

Thus Part 1 of *Messiah* circles back to an old word, *glory*, but in the process bestows on it a new meaning. The Messiah is a king, but not one who relishes gold chariots and crown jewels. Soloists describe instead a king who opens the eyes of the blind and loosens the tongues of the mute, of a king who "shall feed his flock like a shepherd" and "shall gather the lambs with his arm."

For this reason Part 1 can end with a tender, almost paradoxical invitation: "Come unto him, all ye ... that are heavy laden, and he will give you rest. ... His yoke is easy, and his burden is light." The Messiah rules, surely, but he rules with a rod of love. Who may abide the day of his coming? Anyone may abide it; all who come unto him will be welcomed.

During intermission we mingled with other concertgoers, and downed yet another cup of coffee. The drama of Part 1 was working its effect on me, however, even as I traded pleasantries in the lobby. Suddenly it seemed very odd to be sitting so politely as we listened to this earth-shattering story. We should be jumping or clapping hands, like charismatics.

Everyone else seemed quite calm and unperturbed, though, and we found our seats again and prepared for *Messiah*, Part 2. Any listener, no matter how musically naïve, can sense an ominous change in the opening sounds. Handel telegraphs the darkening mood with dense orchestral chords in a minor key, then has the chorus announce it with his ever-significant introductory word, "*Behold* the Lamb of God!" Part 2 describes the world's response to that Messiah born of a virgin, and the story is tragic beyond all telling.

Handel relies mostly on the words of Isaiah 52–53, that remarkably vivid account written centuries before Jesus' birth. All sound ceases for a moment, and after this dramatic pause the contralto, with no accompaniment, gives the disturbing news: "He was de-spis-ed ... re-ject-ed." She pronounces each syllable with great effort, as if the facts of history are too painful to recite. Violins hauntingly reiterate each phrase.

At Calvary, history hung suspended. The bright hopes that had swirled around the long-awaited deliverer of Israel collapsed in darkness that fateful night. Dangling like a scarecrow between two thieves, the Messiah provoked at worst derision, at best pity. "All they that see him laugh him to scorn," says the tenor, who then adds, in the most poignant moment of Handel's oratorio, *"Behold, and see if there be any sorrow like unto his sorrow."*

Yet all is not lost! A few measures later the same tenor introduces the first glimmer of hope: "But thou didst not leave his soul in hell." Almost immediately the whole chorus takes up the shout of joy: "Lift up your heads, O ye gates." For the defeat at Calvary was only an *apparent* defeat. The scarecrow corpse did not remain a corpse. He was the King of Glory after all!

Handel uses the rest of Part 2 to celebrate the triumph wrested from seeming defeat. Nations may rage together, conspiring against peace and justice, but "He that dwelleth in heaven shall laugh them to scorn." The word-play is intentional: he that was laughed to scorn will have the last laugh.

"Hallelujah!" the chorus cries out at last, and from there the music soars into what is unarguably the most famous portion of Handel's *Messiah*, and one of the most jubilant passages of music ever composed. Handel himself said that when he wrote the "Hallelujah!" chorus, "I did think I did see all Heaven before me, and the Great God himself."

Part 1 ends with a scriptural invitation ("Come unto him") based on a paradox; Part 2 explains the paradox of how his yoke can indeed be easy, and his burden light. It is because of a transfer of suffering. At the cross, the pain and sorrow of humanity became the pain and sorrow of God. The chorus early on states it well: "Surely, he hath borne our griefs, and carried our sorrows ... and with his stripes we are healed."

Furthermore, in that act death itself died. What happened next, on the day of resurrection, was a miracle deserving of all praise, deserving of the "Hallelujah!" chorus.

At the London première of *Messiah,* King George I stood for the singing of the "Hallelujah!" chorus. Some skeptics suggest that the king stood to his feet less out of respect for "Hallelujah!" than out of the mistaken assumption that *Messiah* had reached its conclusion.

Even today novices in the audience make the same mistake. Who can blame them? After two hours of performance, the music seems to culminate in the rousing chorus. What more is needed?

I had never really considered the question until that night at the Barbican Centre. But as I glanced at the few paragraphs of libretto remaining, I realized what was missing from Parts 1 and 2. They supply the narrative of Jesus' life, but not the underlying meaning. Part 3 steps out from the story and, gathering quotations from Romans, 1 Corinthians, and Revelation, provides that essential layer of interpretation.

When we flew to England earlier that day, the route took us over the polar ice cap. I knew that beneath the ice cap, nuclear attack submarines prowled, each one capable of killing a hundred million human beings. We landed in London to the news that a train had crashed, killing 51 commuters. Within the week, a terrorist bombed Pan Am flight 103 over Lockerbie, Scotland, killing 270. Is this the world God had in mind at Creation? The world Jesus had in mind at Incarnation?

For reasons such as these, Handel's *Messiah* could not rightly end with the "Hallelujah!" chorus. The Messiah has come in "glory" (Part 1); the Messiah has

died and been resurrected (Part 2). Why, then, does the
world remain in such a sorry state? Part 3 attempts an
answer. Beyond the images from Bethlehem and Calvary,
one more messianic image is needed: the Messiah as
Sovereign Lord. The Incarnation did not usher in the
end of history—only the beginning of the end. Much
work remains before creation is restored to God's original intent.

In a brilliant stroke, Part 3 of *Messiah* opens with a
quotation from Job, that tragic figure who clung stub-
bornly to faith amid circumstances that called for bleak
despair. "I know that my Redeemer liveth, and that he
shall stand at the latter day upon the earth," the soprano
sings out. Overwhelmed by tragedy, with scant evidence
of a sovereign God, Job still managed to believe; and,
Handel implies, so should we.

From that defiant opening, Part 3 shifts to the apostle
Paul's theological explanation of Christ's death ("Since
by man came death ...") and then moves quickly to his
lofty words about a final resurrection ("The trumpet
shall sound, and the dead shall be raised").

Just as the tragedy of Good Friday was transformed
into the triumph of Easter Sunday, one day all war,
all violence, all injustice, all sadness will likewise be

transformed. Then and only then we will be able to say, "O death, where is thy sting? O grave, where is thy victory?" The soprano carries that thought forward to its logical conclusion, quoting from Romans 8: "If God be for us, who can be against us?" If we believe, truly believe, that the last enemy has been destroyed, then we indeed have nothing to fear. At long last, death is swallowed up in victory.

Handel's masterwork ends with a single scene frozen in time. To make his point about the Christ of eternity, librettist Jennens could have settled on the scene from Revelation 2, where Jesus appears with a face like the shining sun and eyes like blazing fire. Instead, his text concludes with the scene from Revelation 4–5, perhaps the most vivid image in a book of vivid imagery.

Twenty-four impressive rulers are gathered together, along with four living creatures who represent strength and wisdom and majesty—the best in all creation. These creatures and rulers kneel respectfully before a throne luminous with lightning and encircled by a rainbow. An angel asks who is worthy to break a seal that will open up the scroll of history. Neither the creatures nor the 24 rulers are worthy. The author realizes well the significance of that moment, "I wept and wept because no one was found who was worthy to open the scroll or look inside."

Besides these creatures, impotent for the grand task, one more creature stands before the throne. Though appearance offers little to recommend him, he is nevertheless history's sole remaining hope. "Then I saw a Lamb, looking as if it had been slain." A lamb! A helpless, baa-baa lamb, and a slaughtered one at that! Yet John in Revelation, and Handel in *Messiah,* sum up all history in this one mysterious image. The great God who became a baby, who became a lamb, who became a sacrifice—this God, who bore our stripes and died our death, this one alone is worthy. That is where Handel leaves us, with the chorus "Worthy Is the Lamb," followed by exultant amens.

We were sitting in a modern brick-and-oak auditorium in the late twentieth century in a materialistic culture light years removed from the imagery of slaughtered lambs. But Handel understood that history and civilization are not what they appear. Auditoriums, dynasties, civilizations—all rise and fall. History has proven beyond doubt that nothing fashioned by the hand of humanity will last. We need something greater than history, something outside history. We need a Lamb slain before the foundations of the world.

I confess that belief in an invisible world, a world beyond this one, does not come easily for me. Like many moderns, I sometimes wonder if reality ends with the material world around us, if life ends at death, if history ends with annihilation or solar exhaustion. But that evening I had no such doubts. Jet lag and fatigue had produced in me something akin to an out-of-body state, and for that moment the grand tapestry woven by Handel's music seemed more real by far than my everyday world. I felt I had a glimpse of the grand sweep of history. And all of it centered in the Messiah who came on a rescue mission, who died on that mission, and who wrought from that death the salvation of the world. I went away with renewed belief that he (and we) shall indeed reign forever and ever.

It was a good decision after all, attending this serendipitous concert.

✷

The Invasion of God

Charles Colson with Anne Morse

Christmas controversies have become as seasonal as candy canes and eggnog. Last year's flap over Wal-Mart forbidding its employees to wish customers "Merry Christmas" reveals how absurd the battles have become.

Christian legal societies stay busy each holiday season, holding the line. But in focusing on the public battles, we may miss a less visible danger in our own ranks.

What image does the mention of Christmas typically conjure up? For most of us, it's a babe lying in a manger while Mary and Joseph, angels and assorted beasts, look on. It's a heartwarming picture—Jesus in swaddling clothes. But Christmas is about much more than a child's birth—even the Savior's birth. It is about the Incarnation: God himself, Creator of heaven and earth, the ultimate reality, becoming flesh.

This is a staggering thought. The Jews believed the Messiah would arrive as a king on a stallion with a flashing sword. But God, who delights in confounding worldly wisdom, dealt with Satan's cruel reign with a quiet invasion of planet Earth. Instead of sending a mighty army, he chose an unknown, teenage virgin.

Thirty years after his humble birth, Jesus increased the Jews' befuddlement when he told his followers, "The time has come. ... The kingdom of God is near. Repent and believe the good news" (Mark 1:15 NIV).

Then he read from the book of Isaiah: "The Spirit of the Lord is upon me, because he anointed me to preach the gospel to the poor ... to proclaim release to the captives, and recovery of sight to the blind, to set free those who are downtrodden ..." Then Jesus closed the book and announced: "Today this Scripture is fulfilled in your hearing" (Luke 4:21 NIV).

In effect, the carpenter's son had just announced that *he* was the king—an outrageous claim to the Jews, and so radical that people wanted to kill him that very day.

Sometimes I think Jesus' announcement of the liberation of the Jewish people and the coming of God's kingdom is as misunderstood today as it was by the Jews of his time. Christ was bringing in the reign of God on earth; first, through his own ministry, and then by establishing a peaceful occupying force—his church—which would carry on God's redeeming work until Christ's return in power and glory and the kingdom's final triumph.

As I've written in my forthcoming book, *The Faith Given Once, for All*, Jesus' announcement was the decisive moment in the whole of human history. Preoccupied with self and distracted by affluence, many Christians try to confine the gospel to a superior form of therapy; they fail to see it as a cosmic plan of redemption in which they, as fallen creatures, are directly involved.

But while the average Christian may not "get" this announcement, those locked behind bars certainly do.

Whenever I've preached to inmates over the last 32 years, I've read Jesus' inaugural sermon. When I quote his promise of freedom for the prisoners, the inmates often raise their arms and cheer. Jesus' message means freedom and victory for those who once had no hope. They aren't distracted by the encumbrance of wealth.

People in the developing world "get it," too. Whenever I share these words with poor, oppressed people in foreign lands, I see eyes brightening.

They understand that Jesus came to proclaim a new kingdom, which is one reason why Christianity is exploding in the Global South. People stripped of every material blessing and exploited by earthly powers long for Christ's bold new kingdom. He turns the world upside down.

It's no wonder that those opposed to Jesus' rule ordered him crucified. He was a threat to the established order and the champion of everyone who acknowledged their imprisonment to sin.

As I like to tell prisoners, Jesus was "busted," betrayed by a "snitch," and sent to death row, utterly rejected. He was strip-searched and then died on the cross between two thieves, so that we could be freed from the grip of Satan and death.

This Christmas, go ahead and decorate your tree and arrange the figures of your creche. But do so in the light of this beautiful and earth-shaking truth: the birth of the baby in the manger was the thrilling signal that God had invaded planet Earth.

Christianity won't rise or fall on whether Wal-Mart employees can say "Merry Christmas." But its future does depend, in part, on how God's people advance God's kingdom, as we help establish his peaceful rule in the present historical moment, until Christ reigns in all his glory.

That we do this is my prayer for Christmas.

✴

Saved by the Bell

Verne Becker

On a Saturday morning in December, I look down from the window of my high-rise apartment in Printers' Row, a quasi-renaissance neighborhood in the South Loop of Chicago. The temperature outside is zero. Vapors rise from every nook and cranny of the cityscape. The El train creaks and squeals more than usual as it slowly passes on its steel trestle. Pedestrians swaddled in heavy overcoats and scarves lean into the biting wind as they scurry for the warmth of their cars or condos.

To the left, I notice a few men on State Street who are not hurrying anywhere: they are merely standing on the corner, hands in pockets, some without hats, enduring the cold. They are homeless. What do they do on days like today?

All I know is that I'd rather be anywhere today than on Chicago's frigid streets. But that is exactly where I am headed. I have volunteered to do something I never thought I'd do: stand outside and ring the bell for the Salvation Army. I'm scheduled for five hours—11 to 4. The big chill.

My first image of the Salvation Army comes from when I was six. Outside the entrance to Sears, during the Christmas season, stood a man wearing a uniform. He looked something like a policeman, but he rang a bell while people walked up and put money into a red bucket. Mom told me the money was to help people who didn't have enough food to eat or clothes to wear. I had never met anyone like that, but I nevertheless enjoyed putting a quarter into the kettle.

As a teenager during the late sixties and early seventies, I, along with millions of other young Americans, developed a strong distaste for all things military—even things that sounded military. I had no idea who the holiday bell-ringers really were, but I certainly didn't want to give my support to anyone whose name ended in *army*.

But over the years I have picked up scattered bits of information about the Salvation Army. Adolescent suspicion has been replaced by adult respect.

I learned that the Salvation Army is a Christian organization—a denomination, in fact—which, unlike (for example) the YMCA in this country, had never abandoned its evangelical roots. William Booth founded the group as an evangelistic street ministry in England in 1865. Fifteen years later, George Scott Railton invaded Battery Park in New York City with six "Hallelujah Lassies," organized street meetings, and opened a storefront outreach in Brooklyn. The first kettles appeared in San Francisco in 1891, when Army Captain Joseph McFee raised funds to provide Christmas dinners for the families of shipwrecked seamen.

The Army's unique mix of evangelism and social programs continued throughout this century, with evangelism remaining paramount. The Army still conducts weekly services (complete with invitations to receive Christ) at its community centers all over the country. While community centers act like churches, their distinctive mission is to meet the physical and spiritual needs of the poor and downtrodden.

My corner is just outside the main entrance to Marshall Field's department store at State and Washington Streets. All around the store, shivering shoppers cluster in front of the famous Christmas windows, looking at lavish scenes in which mechanical figurines of elves, Santas, children, animals, and Dickensian characters gesture and dance. Right next to the empty stand that marks my spot is a Salvation Army window, with Santa ringing a bell and children putting money in the red kettle. A perfect location.

A thin man in his fifties walks up and tells me he's the supervisor for the Loop ringers. "You must be from the accounting firm," he says.

I explain that I merely called in and volunteered to ring, and was told to go to this corner.

"That's funny," he says. "A big firm signed up to handle kettles today, and not a one of them has shown up."

"How many ringers do you have altogether?"

On a typical day during the holiday season, he explains, 16 people work the Chicago Loop streets. Nine of them are paid a minimum wage by the Salvation Army; usually they come from one of the Army's social-service programs or rehabilitation centers. The other seven, the Army hopes, are covered by volunteers—such as the ones who didn't show up today. I notice that the kettles for paid workers are locked to the stands, while volunteers can remove and carry their own.

When the supervisor leaves to check on the other kettles, I realize my time has come: I take a deep breath and start ringing. For some reason, I feel embarrassed. Maybe it's because I've often felt funny when I passed a bell-ringer, thinking he was a street beggar or a member of a strange religious sect.

While I fret about my self-image and how I "come off" in public, a little girl of three or four walks up and drops some change in the kettle. The girl's mother looks at me with a smile and says, "It was her idea."

The surge of feeling I experience surprises me. When the next few contributors walk up, I find I can't speak: They too are children. Perhaps children have the fewest inhibitions to overcome about giving. They don't cross-examine their motives. They don't really care how they appear to others, or worry about their social graces. But at this moment I am struck by their free and gracious spirit.

In a matter of minutes, I not only feel relaxed, but I actually begin to enjoy myself. I ring my bell to various cadences, alternating between ding-ding, ding-ding, ding-ding, and the more complex shave-and-a-haircut rhythm: ding-dinga-ding-ding, a-ding-ding. All the while throngs of vapor-breathing shoppers pass by, toting their children wrapped up like packages. Many of them—young and old, rich and poor—pause for a moment to drop a few coins or stuff a few bills into my bucket. Everyone is friendly, especially the children, and their warmth more than compensates for the bitter temperature.

I notice that many kids take the initiative to nudge their parents and say, "Can I put some money in?" Other times the parents pull out some change and hand it to the child to put in. I cannot help believing those parents are teaching their kids something positive about the value of giving.

Before long I am greeting people and joking with the children. Many of them are so tightly bound in coats and scarves that they look like mini-mummies: I see nothing but two little blue eyes.

"Hi in there!" I say. Some of them are shy, but many laugh and look right at me, unlike most of the adults.

One little girl of about seven walks up and asks, "Why are you standing here?"

"Well, I'm collecting money to give to people who can't afford to have a nice Christmas, so they can have a nice Christmas, too."

"You mean poor people?"

"That's right—poor people."

"OK," she says, apparently satisfied, and puts in some change. "Here. Merry Christmas."

As the shadows lengthen on the street, I glance at my watch and can hardly believe it's already 3:30. I'm having such a good time that I don't want to stop. And so many people are giving that I think, *If I stay here 15 more minutes, that could mean another 15 or 20 dollars.* But I decide to quit, since the kettle drop-off location will be closing soon.

Just before I leave, a tightly bundled boy of nine or ten walks up with a tattered plastic grocery bag. "Do you have any use for these?" he says, holding the bag open. Inside I see a teddy bear and a coloring book.

"You mean you want to give them to me?" I say, flustered. I don't see the kid's parents anywhere. And the supervisor hadn't told me how to handle anything but money. I consider telling him thanks, but I can't accept anything that won't fit in the slot.

But then I think for a moment. "Thank you very much," I say at last. "I'm sure I can find someone who would love these gifts. I'd be happy to take them." The little boy smiles and strolls away.

I am the last one to arrive back at the office to drop everything off. The paid ringers sit on folding chairs around the perimeter of the room and smoke. The supervisor thanks me, sticks my kettle in a safe, and locks it. When I hand him the bear and the coloring book, he says, "Sure, we can use those—no problem." Then everyone stands to leave.

Listening to the conversations in the elevator, I realize that these men aren't going home to luxury high-rise dwellings. One of them says something about being an alcoholic. Another says he hopes the landlord had turned the heat back on in his building. It occurs to me that it is these people, and others in similar situations, that the money in my kettle goes to help.

As I head south on State Street, back to my cushy apartment, I once again pass those familiar homeless faces in my neighborhood. Perhaps the money I collected will help some of them, too. But then I think, *Get serious,*

Verne—just how much of a difference are you going to make in these people's lives with a few hours of bell-ringing?

Maybe none, at least not directly. But I have to believe that the bell-ringing of thousands of others like me all across the country will indeed make some kind of difference. Today I realize even a small step in the direction of helping those who really need help is better than no step at all.

In my four-and-a-half hours of ringing, I probably raised $150. But something else is raised, too: my own faith in human nature. After watching so many people, rich and poor, old and young, joyfully giving even the smallest amount of change to help the needy, I can't help but think that in spite of all the materialism, decadence, and selfishness in the world, there remains in all of us at least a fragment of the image of a giving God. And it is that fragment that the Salvation Army appeals to, and nurtures, at Christmas and throughout the year.

✧

His Kingdom Is Forever

D. Martyn Lloyd-Jones

And in the days of these kings shall the God of heaven set up a kingdom, which shall never be destroyed ... it shall break in pieces and consume all these kingdoms, and it shall stand for ever. (Dan 2:44 KJV)

And it came to pass in those days that there went out a decree from Caesar Augustus that all the world should be taxed. (Luke 2:1 KJV)

King Nebuchadnezzar has had that dream which Daniel alone was able to recall and to interpret. Now the precise time when all this happened was this: the children of Israel, because of their sins, had been conquered by Babylon and carried away into captivity. Jerusalem had been destroyed, the Temple was in ruins, and all that Israel had prided herself on, in a sense, lay there in desolate and hopeless condition. The land was derelict and the Israelites captives, indeed slaves, under the domination of Nebuchadnezzar. It was one of the lowest points in the history of Israel. They were the people of God, the people to whom God had made his promises, but here they were in this miserable and seemingly hopeless condition. But it was just there and then, in such a situation, that this tremendous thing happened and this message was given to them, full of hope and bright future, full of a certainty which nothing could remove and destroy.

Here is something thoroughly typical of God's method, something that runs through the Bible as a recurring theme, even at the very beginning in Genesis. Watch those men on whom God had set his affections; constantly he allows them to get into some hopeless position. There they are feeling utterly disconsolate and their enemies are full of a sense of triumph and of rejoicing. But suddenly God comes in and the whole situation is changed.

Now that has always been God's method, and it is an essential part of the message of the Christian faith, illustrated most perfectly of all in the coming of the Son of God into the world. When the Lord Jesus was born into this world, once more the situation was completely hopeless. Since the prophet Malachi there had been no word from God, as it were; for 400 long years there had been no true prophet in Israel. God seemed to be silent. The children of Israel seemed to be abandoned, and their country conquered by Rome. It was into that kind of situation, when it was least expected, that God did the greatest thing of all—he sent his only begotten Son into the world to rescue and redeem men.

That is the great thing that stands out in the whole history of the Christian Church; and that is why this message is of such comfort and strength to Christian people at the present time. How often the Christian Church has seemed to be at the very end of its tether—lifeless, helpless and hopeless. Her enemies had become loud, proud and arrogant, convinced that Christianity was finished; the doors of the churches seemed about to be shut for the last time. A bleak midwinter had settled upon the Church, and then suddenly and quite unexpectedly God sent a mighty and glorious revival. That message stands out on the very surface, and is quite clear in this prophecy. The prophecy was fulfilled literally and it has continued to be fulfilled in principle ever since. Therefore as we look at ourselves today and see the Christian Church as but a dwindling remnant in this sinful, arrogant world, and many begin to feel hopeless and anxious about the future—here is the message of God. It has been God's custom throughout the centuries to come and visit his people when they least expect it. Who knows but that round the corner there may be waiting for us a mighty and glorious revival of religion! Let us take hold of this great principle.

Now let us come to a consideration of the message itself, for it is full of the most extraordinary things. First of all God gives here a prophecy of the exact time his Son is going to be born into this world: "And in the days of these kings shall the God of heaven set up a kingdom ..." The dream indicated that there was going to be a succession of kingdoms. First of all this head of gold, which Daniel told him in the interpretation was Nebuchadnezzar himself, and the kingdom of Babylon. That was going to be followed by a kingdom of silver—the Medo-Persian dynasty, that in turn was to be replaced by a kingdom of brass—the kingdom of Greece, Alexander the Great, so called. And that was to be followed by this kingdom of iron with its divisions and the admixture of clay as well—and that is, of course, the Roman Empire.

Then we are told that when the Roman Empire would be in the fullness of its sway and its sovereignty, God was going to set up his Kingdom, was going to send his Son as King to start this mighty Kingdom of Heaven. And so, that first verse in Luke 2 tells us that it actually happened at that time: "And it came to pass in those days that there went out a decree from Caesar Augustus." Here we have one of those numerous instances of the particularity of Old Testament prophecy. It does not merely prophesy the coming of the Son of God into the world generally and vaguely; it tells us the exact time. Later on, in the ninth chapter of this Book of Daniel, it is still more particular and fixes the very year when He was to come. Micah tells us that he was to be born in Bethlehem, and so on. Notice the particularity, and let us draw the great lesson from it, that God is controlling history. It was when "the fulness of the times was come" that God "sent forth his Son made of a woman, made under the law, to redeem them that were under the law."

Let us look at the characteristics of the Kingdom—and here, as we do so, we shall see a summary of the Gospel. The thing emphasized is that this Kingdom is going to be essentially different from all other kingdoms. In what respects? First, it is not going to rise out of any one of the other kingdoms. It is a kingdom that will arise independently, apart from, entirely distinct from the others. You remember that in the case of the earthly kingdoms, each arose out of the ruins of the previous one. A great conqueror came and conquered and demolished the previous kingdom, set up his own on the foundation of the former. And that happened to each in turn.

But God's Kingdom is not going to be like that, it does not belong to that order at all. Let us never forget, therefore, that this dream image of Nebuchadnezzar not only describes those four kingdoms and empires, but it typifies and represents all earthly, human, worldly power. But this other Kingdom does not belong to that order. That is why our Lord said to Pontius Pilate, "My Kingdom is not of this world." It is a spiritual Kingdom, an unseen Kingdom, a Kingdom in the hearts of men. That is God's Kingdom. It does not belong to the image seen by Nebuchadnezzar.

Let me point out something still more wonderful. It is a Kingdom that presents a striking contrast in its lowliness and in its apparent insignificance. It is compared to "a stone cut out without hands." You see at once this striking contrast. The kingdoms of the world are great and wonderful in their pomp and majesty, their external show and all their glory—gold, silver, brass, iron! And then there is this other little kingdom—a common stone!

What a perfect description of the Kingdom of God! We must never lose sight of this. It is an essential part of the Bible's message. The children of Israel seemed so small and insignificant in their origin. Israel was a very small country, and when you contrast her with these great empires, how insignificant she always seemed to be.

But that is not really the thing to emphasize. Look what happened when God's Son came into this world. Where was he born? It was not in a king's palace, not in purple, not surrounded by gold and silver and brass. Born in a stable, placed in a manger—a stone! Born into a very poor family that could not afford to sacrifice a lamb, they could only buy turtle doves. There was nothing more humble and more lowly. It is all in that picture of the stone. It shows us the humble origin of our Lord as born in the flesh: the insignificance of his position, because he was not a Pharisee and had never been to the schools; the insignificance of his kingdom, just followed by a rabble of ordinary, common people; spending most of his time in Galilee and not in the capital, nor in Jerusalem and in

Judea. There it is, the stone contrasted with the gold and the silver and the brass and the iron.

What conclusion must we draw from all this? Hear the author of the Epistle to the Hebrews: "Wherefore, we receiving a Kingdom which cannot be moved, let us have grace and let us be steadfast ..." The thing that matters is that we belong to this Kingdom. The kingdoms of this world, whatever form they may take—whether military, or social, or political, or philosophical—talk about the gold, the silver, the brass and the iron. Exalt them as you will, they are all going to be destroyed. Listen: "Forasmuch as thou sawest that the stone was cut out of the mountain without hands, and that it brake in pieces the iron, the brass, the clay, the silver and the gold, the great God hath made known to the king what shall come to pass hereafter. And the dream is certain, and the interpretation thereof sure."

I ask you this personal question: Are you a citizen of this Kingdom which cannot be destroyed, whose power shall never pass to another? Do you know that you are reconciled to God by the blood of Christ? Have you been made anew? Not by the hands of man, or man's manipulation or understanding, but by the hands of God? Have you experienced the second birth? Have you "the author-ity" to become a son of God? Are you born "not of blood nor of the will of the flesh, nor of the will of man, but of God"? If so, you are in the Kingdom and you will remain in it though the whole world rock and shake in the con-vulsion of an Armageddon. You are secure because you belong to a Kingdom which never can be moved. Blessed be the God and Father of our Lord Jesus Christ, who hath visited and redeemed his people.

✶

Painting Christmas

Walter Wangerin, Jr.

A plain photograph of the birth of Jesus would be altogether unremarkable—except that it showed a woman bearing her baby in a public place. That might cause a remark or two. Polite society could find the photo offensive ("Rifraff, as shameless of private bodily functions as the homeless in New York City"). Social activists could criticize polite society itself ("Don't blame the victim! Bearing babies in stables is a sign of the country's unkindness").

But no one would call the photo holy.

That which the camera could record of the nativity of Jesus does not inspire awe. It is either too common or too impoverished. A cold, modern scrutiny, a searching of the surface of things, reveals nothing much meaningful here.

Let me put it another way: If, for us, reality is material only; if we gaze at the birth with that modern eye which acknowledges nothing spiritual, sees nothing divine, demands the hard facts only, data, documentation; if truth for us is merely empirical, then we are left with a photograph of small significance: a derelict husband, an immodest mother, a baby cradled in a feed-trough in an outdoor shelter for pack animals—a lean-to, likely, built behind a mud-brick house where travelers slept both on the floor within and on the roof without. Simple, rude, dusty, and bare.

Ah, but those for whom this is the only way to gaze at Christmas must themselves live lives bereft of meaning: nothing spiritual, nothing divine, no awe, never a gasp of adoration, never the sense of personal humiliation before glory *nor* the shock of personal exaltation when Glory chooses also to bow down and to love.

Such people have chosen a shell-existence, hollow at the core. Today, a fruitless rind; tomorrow, quintessential dust.

Our seeing reveals our soul—whether we conceive of one or not. So how do we see Christmas?

If we do not recognize in the person of this infant an act of almighty God who here initiates forgiveness for this rebellious world; if we do not see in Jesus the Word made baby flesh, nor honor him as the only premise for any Christmas celebration, then we see with that modern eye merely. Stale, flat, unprofitable.

If the "true meaning of Christmas" is for us some vague sentiment of fellowship and charity and little else, then we see with that modern eye merely. Human goodness is a poor alternative to *Immanuel*, the active, personal presence of God among us. Human goodness is unstable. God is not. Moreover, to celebrate human goodness is to celebrate ourselves—and there never was a self that could elevate itself by staring at the self alone. Mirrors are always experienced on exactly the same level as oneself, neither higher nor lower.

If the "spirit of the season" is for us a harried getting and spending, an exchanging of gifts, we see with that modern eye merely. Instead of the love of God to redeem us from dying (and so to cause in us his ever-living love), we have that halting human love that might redeem a day from loneliness but that itself must, at the end of that day, die.

Or if we reduce the glory of the Incarnation to craven phrases like "Season's Greetings" (for fear of offending some customer, some boss, some someone who finds no Christ in Christmas), then we offend God by bowing down before those who see with the modern eye merely. Likewise, "Peace!" is rendered an empty wish and "Joy!" is sourceless if ever we are ashamed of the Prince of Peace. For the world can make an illusion of joy, but illusions, when they shatter against experience, leave people worse than before. And this world has never, never, by its own wisdom and strength, compacted a lasting peace.

No. I will not see the scene with that empirical, modern eye. I refuse to accept the narrow sophistications and dead-eyed adulthoods of a "realistic" world. I choose to stay a child. My picture shall not be undimensioned, therefore, neither as flat as a photograph nor as cold as news copy—no, never as cold as my scientist's case study.

Rather, I will paint my picture with baby awe, wide-eyed, primitive, and faithful. More medieval than modern.

More matter than material. And I will call it true: for it sees what is but is not seen. It makes the invisible obvious.

My painting is immense. Stand back to look at it. It is composed of seven concentric circles, each one lesser than the last, and all surrounding Jesus.

Orbis primus. The widest circle is the whole world, dark and cold and winterfast. The universe. All creation yearning for this birth and all of it mute until a word is put within its mouth. This word: In the beginning was the Word, and the Word was with God, and the Word was God. That one.

Orbis secundus. Just inside the first sphere is another, scarcely smaller than the first because it touches that one everywhere and serves the whole of it. The second is a choir of angels countless as the stars, bright with white light and expectation, gazing inward, full of news—for heaven itself attends his Advent here!

Orbus tertius. The third circle is trees, great ancient trees, the giants that stand in shadow outside civilization, northern forest, the jungle that ruins every human road, mountain escarpments covered with timber, the cedars of Lebanon—for it is from the simplest growing things that the beams and boards of the Lord's rude birthing-room is built. The third circle is poor and dark and huge with groaning. When you hear it, you might call that sound the wind; I tell you, it is the travail of trees long ago made subject unto vanity, who even now await with eager longing the manifestation of the Son of God.

Of these trees is fashioned a stable—order emerging from the wild world. But the stable lacks all sign of wealth. It offers no comfort of civilized life. For this King shall be lowborn in order to lift the low on high. The abandoned, the rejected, those that sit outside the gates—trees and slaves and the poor—shall be delivered from bondage and lifted to the glory and liberty of the children of God!

Orbis quartus. Next are animals, herds and flocks afoot, great streams of obedient beasts and the untamed, too, circling though the midnight forest, gazing inward like the angels, yearning to know the fate of their young: for there are ewes here whose lambs have gone inside the stable; there are cows whose calves are representing the whole species; and there is a donkey whose daughter has borne a woman to the very center of the universe, a woman great with child.

For nature makes a harmony at this Nativity. Fur and feather and human flesh, myriad shapes and yet more myriad voices. Listen! Listen with the ears of your faith and hear in the roaring of all creatures a choral praise and piety, the melody of the turning earth and the music of the spheres: *"Blessing and honor," they sing, "and glory and power be unto him that sitteth upon the throne and unto the Lamb forever and ever!"*

And the lesser lambs and the oxen and that singular donkey say, *"Amen."*

Orbis quintus. The circle in the circle of the singing animals is a gathering of shepherds whom I paint with the faces of children, smiling, shining, breathless, and reverent. You can see their expressions. There is a lantern in this more intimate space, a single flame, and orange light. Warmth. Fire.

These are the people of every age who, hearing the news, believe it. Of course they are children! These are those who, believing the good news, rushed to see it for themselves and have now come in from deepest darkness—through the circles of angels and trees and beasts—to behold with their own eyes a Savior, their Savior, their dear One, their Lord.

Some of the shepherds hold hands. Two are giggling. One weeps. She can't help it. It is what she does when she encounters joy—she weeps.

And one near the back of the bunch is called Wally.

That's me.

Orbis sextus. Circle six is a man and a woman, one standing, one reclined in weariness. The man is Joseph, the stepfather who lends house and heart and lineage to his foster child. The woman is Mary, the mother, regal and transcendently beautiful, for heaven crossed all the circles to choose her; and she, when heaven came near nine months ago, said, "Let it be."

Immediately upon her faithful response it did begin to be!

It happened! It happens still because it happened once.

Ah, children, the sixth circle must be the circle composed of time: the year in the middle of all years, the first day of that year. For this woman's riding on one daughter of the donkeys; for her lying down on straw, her straining forward to bear a King and crying out in dear pain her own verse of the universal hymn; for the crowning of her baby, the infant-skull pressing against the deeps of her most human womanhood—all this is the beginning of the meaning in the history of humankind.

For it is this that keeps creation from the annihilations of absurdity, that on a particular day, in a particular place, within the womb of a particular woman, the fullness of God was pleased to rise through human flesh to be born as flesh himself into the world.

It happened! She brought forth her firstborn son, and wrapped him in swaddling clothes, and—

Orbis septimus.—and the smallest circle of seven, meaner than the others, is a manger of wood.

Wood, lumber from the forests: for Jesus is born material truly, bone and flesh and a red-running blood.

But wood, rough planks hewn by human hands: for one day wood will kill him.

Wood is the bracket of the earthly existence of the Lord Jesus Christ. Wood is the smallest compass around him, for it is our sinning and his loving—which, taken together, shape the very person of the Christ. This is his personal form both visible and invisible, a servant, a slave, a body obedient unto death.

For here, in a sphere which is the size of any human being, is the truth that cannot be seen but which my painting depicts in an outrageous round of wood as in a carving: his life, enclosed by a cradle and a cross, saves ours thereby. Oh, my dear, you are in the picture, too! Do you see yourself? Kneeling next to Wally? And in your hand, a hammer.

In his tiny baby hand, a nail.

Centrum orbium omnium. But then here, in the perfect center of all my circles and of all the spheres of all the world; here, in the center of all galaxies; in the center of thought and love and human gesture, blazing with light more lovely than sunlight, a light that makes of Mary a madonna, light that can kindle wood to burn a sacred flame, light that cancels in fire your hammer and that shows on your brow even now a crown of life, light that lightens the Gentiles and the deepest pathways of all creatures and the forests once sunk in shadow—

—here, I say, in the center of everything, brightening all things even to the extremes of time and eternity—

—here, himself the center that holds all orbits in one grand and universal dance, is Jesus!

Here! Come and look! Do you see the tiny baby born? Do you see that Infant King? And do you recognize in him *Immanuel*?

Amen, child! O wide-eyed child all filled with awe, amen: for now you are seeing Christmas.

✦

Stars on a Silent Night

Charlotte F. Otten

The city of Nijmegen in the Netherlands lay still in the sleep of morning. The noisy burr of motorbikes and the gentle whirr of bicycles were distinctly absent. All was still and dark on the Saturday morning before Christmas, 1959. All was still, that is, except for four people, four Americans awake and stirring in the Netherlands—Bob and I, and our two young sons.

This was no ordinary Saturday morning for us. Christmas vacation had begun for the boys and we were planning a one-day trip into Germany. Nijmegen is close to the German border, and one may see a great deal on a one-day excursion into it.

But today, the Saturday before Christmas, was to be different. We were not going into Germany to see the Cologne Cathedral with its two graceful spires pointing to the sky. Nor were we going to Düsseldorf, shiny and bright as a new penny. We were going to see three tiny villages in the Ruhr Valley—three drab villages which I'm quite sure many Germans have never heard of, let alone Americans. Who knows or cares about Puffendorf, Ederen, or Linnich when Europe is packed full of magnificent things to see? And why visit unknown villages when you have only 10 months to spend in Europe?

The answer was that these were Bob's 10 months. He had come to the Netherlands as a Fulbright Research Scholar. Naturally we would be seeing the famous sights of Europe, but these three villages in the Ruhr Valley meant something to him, for he had lived in them in 1944—he and the big Army howitzers. Now, after 15 years, he wanted to retrace his war steps; he wanted to see the three villages again.

Furthermore, there was another thing he wanted to see—Margraten. Margraten was the huge American War Cemetery near Maastricht in the Netherlands where one of Bob's friends lay buried. Surely this was destined to be a somber sort of day, this Saturday before Christmas, at least for us.

We finished breakfast quickly, and the four of us took off in our little "foreign" car down the road into the dark December morning.

As we drove along, I looked up at the many stars which were still shining. How close they seemed to be, closer than ever before. Of course we were farther north than ever before. We were in the Netherlands, not Michigan, and these plump stars were Dutch stars in a Dutch sky.

I wished secretly that we were not going to visit war villages and a war cemetery. Why did we have to see such reminders of tragedy? How much more appropriate would it be to go to fine art galleries and look at the famous paintings of the birth of the Prince of Peace. War at Christmas time? No!—Why not think of peace?

Somehow I had remained a stranger to war. True, Bob had spent over three years in the American Army, and 18 months in Europe. But God had blessed our family. We had come out of it all unscathed, and I preferred to forget that the Red Horse of War had ever ridden.

I had had premonitions of what we might see this day. The people in Nijmegen had seen the Red Horse, had heard him tramping through their city night after night, day after day, and they had often told us of the days of terror and depression. We had heard them tell of hunger and cruelty and death; and they always spoke as though it had happened yesterday. One friend told of the following incident. Nijmegen had been liberated by the Americans one day in 1944, and the next day there was a celebration in the bombed-out town square. Her husband had been on his way to the square when suddenly a remaining enemy stepped out from behind a building and threw a large grenade. What was left of her husband was put in a cigar box. And that was the day after Liberation! And so we had heard account after account of the riding of the Red Horse of War.

I knew one thing: I did not want to see the Red Horse of War on the Saturday before Christmas. He would surely destroy the joy and peace of Christmas.

Quietly we rode on toward Puffendorf, Ederen, and Linnich. Gradually the stars disappeared and the dawn came, and by the time it was light we had reached the war area. Burned-out tanks graced the landscape. This was farming and orchard area, but nature had not oblit-erated the marks of war.

Then we saw the villages. Here stood a handful of houses, ugly and scarred. Each one had its deep artil-lery wounds. The Red Horse had been here all right. Over there stood a house, or half a house, I should say, with a family living in the front of it and damaged bricks piled high behind it. A lonely pig could be seen scrounging for food in the debris. All around was evidence of destruction. We thought of the age-old phrase, "They make a desola-tion and they call it peace." Peace was here, silent and joy-less. But this was not the peace of Christmas, the joyful peace of the shepherds who welcomed the Christ-Child.

We rode on. In Ederen we saw the Purple Heart Cor-ner. This corner had been ceaselessly shelled, and count-less American boys had been wounded. Now there was no sound of artillery to shake the countryside. No guns boomed or whistled; no soldier dashed for cover. And yet, although 15 years had elapsed, it seemed as though the Red Horse had just ridden through. We could see men rebuilding one of the houses and using the old wounded bricks.

On we rode in silence. Our thoughts lay too deep for tears. Later we stopped for lunch and then continued our drive along the countryside. But never were we able to forget the three war-scarred villages of the Ruhr—"the Villages of the Red Horse," I called them.

Now we had one more thing to see: Margraten. We crossed the border back into the Netherlands. Our young boys were the first to spot the sign for Margraten, and we turned in.

Until the Saturday before Christmas, 1959, Margraten had meant nothing to me. Now, as we stepped out to look over the grounds, the place overwhelmed me. It was all so green, and so still.

Against the rich green of the grass gleamed the tremendous white stone monument with the names of at least 500 American men engraved upon it, and standing for at least 500 separate sorrows. Their bodies were lying here at Margraten, unidentified, and occupying unknown graves. And around about we saw the white crosses, almost 9000 of them—9000 white crosses on a carpet of green. So intensely white were they and so thick that everything seemed blurred to my eyes. Infantry men were here from the Battle of the Bulge who died that Christmas in 1944, and here were pilots and artillery men. Nine thousand American boys lay in the white and green of Margraten, and yet it all seemed bloody red with the hoofmarks of the Red Horse.

We stood a long time, then climbed into our car and headed toward Nijmegen. Darkness came quickly now; it comes early in December in the Netherlands. And gradually the stars reappeared. Bright and large and seemingly very near, they shone down upon us. Suddenly the meaning of this day, this Saturday before Christmas, came to us. We understood it anew. The birth of the Prince of Peace had a fresh and poignantly beautiful meaning.

As suddenly and unexpectedly as the stars reminded us of the Star of Bethlehem, so suddenly and unexpectedly the darkness, sadness, and desolation slipped out of our hearts. The Star of Bethlehem was truly shining on us and speaking to us. And—strangest of all—the Red Horse was leading us straight to the Prince of Peace.

We began to realize how appropriate the day had been. It was in the world of war that the Prince of Peace was born. We knew that although the Red Horse could ride through the world and trample it under his hoofs, he could never triumph over it. The Prince of Peace had come and would come again, riding on a pure white horse with a Cross in his hand, and he would vanquish the Red Horse forever.

We had seen the Red Horse. But we had also seen in a new and striking way the Prince of Peace. That Saturday before Christmas, 1959, the mild Babe of Bethlehem was transformed into the triumphant Prince of Peace. And we heard great voices saying: "The Kingdoms of this world are become the kingdoms of our Lord, and of his Christ; and he shall reign forever and ever."

When God Came Down

Walter A. Elwell

Christmas speaks to us of God's great plan and power. It tells us that God knew what was best for the world and that he held back until the appointed time when he would act. Countless eyes had closed in faith before the Savior came; many weary backs were bent with age in Herod's day, clinging still to the hope that God would act; many hearts had almost failed for fear that somehow God had forgotten his promises of old.

But God does not forget. He works according to a plan that, because it wells up within his eternal being, has eternity in view and hence is in no hurry. The mystery that surrounds the very nature of God himself is woven into the outworking of his will. We do not know why eons passed before God stepped into the world for our redemption. But when the ages were full to the brim—like the ancient water clock that Paul used as an illustration—at that precise moment, God fulfilled his word and sent his Son (Gal 4:4–5).

Aquinas, commenting on these verses, says, "Two reasons are given why that time was preordained for the coming of Christ. One is taken from His greatness: for since He that was to come was great, it was fitting that men be made ready for His coming by many indications and many preparations. The other is taken from the role of the one coming: for since a physician was to come, it was fitting that before his coming, men should be keenly aware of their infirmity, both as to their lack of knowledge during the Law of nature and as to their lack of virtue during the written Law."

We must never forget that God is in control. When we look around and see the apparent collapse of what is right, we are tempted to doubt. At times we feel that no other generation has had so much reason to despair. But faith has always had to rise above the tangled fears that seek to drag it into the pit. Christmas speaks across the years to quiet doubt, remove despair, and vanquish fear.

God rules the world; he does not forget his promises. He works his will as surely as day follows night, and when the time of his appointment came, his will was done. At Christmas God seized control of history and Ultimate Good came down.

The angels, who were sent by God to make the day known, understood God's power. They gladly rushed to do his will, knowing that true strength comes from acting according to God's will. To ride the crest of God's mighty will as it rolls through time is to find the power of God beneath us, lifting us above the anxieties and uncertainties that lurk below. The angels made this known when they announced that in the city of David a Savior was born.

Christmas also speaks to us of the God who works miraculously among us. The coming of Christ to earth was miracle, pure and simple. Such things cannot be and yet it happened because we are dealing not with mere human forecast or probability but with none other than the God of heaven and earth. He spoke and the world came into being; he spoke again and Mary brought forth her first-born son and laid him in a manger.

It is equally important to observe the method of God's miraculous work. He could have acted quite apart from the creation he had made. It would, in fact, have involved God in far less risk. Our history does not exactly commend us as wholly reliable partners in such a momentous event. What of Mary? What of Joseph? What of all those who would have a part in the earthly life of God-made-man? The risk of such a venture would almost seem to cast doubt upon the wisdom of the plan. But God carried through his choice to become one of us by human instrumentality. Frail Mary's flesh became the means used by God to make his entrance into the world. Frail human flesh would then become one with God, without compromise on either part, in what would be the mystery of the Incarnation.

The gain was worth the price of risk. Mankind could now look upon its own despised fragility and no longer weep. That God chose to become one with us meant that we have hope. Our dying frames now may sing with joy; our weariness takes new heart; our sin-weakened lives may shake free the dust that threatens to bury us. God deigned to take upon himself our infirmities, thus sanctifying our human condition, so we can live again. He ate as we eat, he walked as we walk, he lived as we live, he wept as we weep, and he died as we must die. So we may take new heart and live while life's short candle burns as those who once had God among us, sharing our life with us.

What is the essence of Christmas, after all is said and done? Is it just that human flesh knew God and therefore we should rejoice? Important as that is, Christmas means something much deeper: *God,* the King of Kings and Lord of Lords, eternal through the ages, entered into human flesh. There are no words to speak of such a fathomless design. *God himself* is with us. None other. Augustine tried to capture this mystery:

> He it is by whom all things were made, and who was made one of all things; who is the revealer of the Father, the creator of the Mother; the Son of God by the Father without a mother, the Son of man by the Mother without a father; the Word who is God before all time, the Word made flesh at a fitting time, the maker of the sun, made under the sun; ordering all the ages from the bosom of the Father, hallowing a day of to-day from the womb of the Mother; remaining in the former, coming forth from the latter; author of the heaven and the earth, sprung under the heaven out of the earth; unutterably wise, in His wisdom a babe without utterance; filling the world, lying in a manger.

Mark the greatness of divine humility. In taking on human flesh, he took on all the frailness of our weakened state. He made himself vulnerable and open to attack. He clearly knew what this would mean, but his purposes required such a condescension. Again, Augustine says: "O food and bread of Angels, the Angels are filled by Thee, but Where art Thou for my sake? In a mean lodging, in a manger. He who rules the stars, sucks at the breast; He who speaks in the bosom of the Father, is silent in the Mother's lap. But He will speak when He reaches suitable age, and will fulfill for us the gospel. For our sakes He will suffer, for us He will die; as an example of our reward He will rise again; He will ascend into heaven before the eyes of His disciples, and He will come from heaven to judge the world. Behold Him lying in the manger; He is reduced to tininess, yet He has not lost anything of Himself; He has accepted what was not His, but He remains what He was. Thus behold the infant Christ."

Why would God allow himself to be "reduced to tininess"? He was moved by love—love for his lost creation. We do not know why that should be. We only know that on that night Eternity came down into time for us, in order to lift us back into eternity with him. Such ever was love's way; to rise, it stoops and we gaze in silent wonder before it, trying to grasp its full significance. Love was made a man, and from that man there shines a light into the darkness of our world that bids all sorrow flee and all anxiety depart.

But love is vulnerable and not even God's love is exempt from that. To come to earth meant going the full distance and feeling the full measure of our humanity, even unto death. Death's slow tolling bell rang when Mary heard the shepherds' words and pondered them darkly in her heart. Love brought God down to earth and love would drive him deeper still. The sin of all the world would be upon him on the cross, who now in wordless infancy cried softly in the manger.

Finally, Christmas can challenge us today: because Christmas was, we cannot stay the same. What Christmas means in concrete human terms is as plain as the manger, the shepherds, the angels, and the cross.

It means, first of all, that we must walk in full recognition of God's overall triumphant plan and will. He who planned the ages and even submitted unto that plan himself has a plan for this age too. We should not chafe to do his will, but delight in it, as Mary or the angels at that first Christmas. The way to sure defeat lies in the substitution of our proud wills for the will of God himself.

Let us follow the example of all of those who saw God's will and did it.

Second, Christmas means we are called to look on human life as sanctified and of great worth to God. God did not despise the flesh he made, nor must we. Nor are we to value our own flesh above that of others. God came into *flesh,* not *our* flesh alone. God cares for every human soul, born and yet unborn. Our care should extend to every human soul—the weak, the sick, the suffering, and the defenseless. Because God cared enough about human life to become a part of it, we cannot despise part of it, lest we be despising God himself.

Third, Christmas calls us to accept a life of vulnerability and simplicity in the face of God's acceptance of our weak estate. He set the pattern for us. We cannot strive for power or wealth at the expense of someone else. We must follow Christ upon the road from heaven to earth to cross, and leave the rest to God. The whole world is not worth our soul, and Christmas says, behold the one who, though he was rich, became poor for our sakes. So must we also live.

Fourth, Christmas calls us to make the love of God real in humble, loving service. Just as God stooped down, so must we stoop. This should not be misunderstood: it was not weakness in God that sent him down to earth, but rather strength. He voluntarily laid aside the glory. So, too, it is not weakness to walk in humble submission to God's will in willing service to others, no matter what the world thinks. It is a triumph and a victory in our lives when we walk in humility, after the pattern of the Ultimate Good come down.

The turning point of history was Christmas; may it be the turning point in our lives this year.

✧

On the Festival of Christ's Nativity

Thomas Howard

The most astounding and the most familiar story of all is the story of the Nativity. And this very familiarity may give us trouble, from time to time. We feel as though we ought to be perpetually awestruck by a tale of such wonders; we hold it to be *true*. But we find that we can rehearse the whole thing, just as we can rehearse the events of the Passion, and not really be "moved" by it. What is wrong? Are we so cloddish that we can speak of God with us, and of such marvels as the Virgin Mother and archangels and the star, without being profoundly moved every time?

The notion that we ought to be so moved fails to take into account one big psychological datum, and it is this: we human beings cannot remain for very long in *any* highly intense frame of mind, whether it be grief or joy or awe or anger or whatever. That is, no matter what the original stimulus may have been that aroused the feelings, we find that, after the first flush, there is a pattern of receding and surging, and that the crest does not stay fixed at some high point. We find a respite, and then perhaps a return periodically to the intensity of feeling.

Anyone who has experienced a death close at hand knows this. The grief is there, but the wild surges of uncontrollable feeling come only at irregular intervals. Or joy: we don't remain for long, steady periods in any elevated state of tingling bliss. It comes and goes. And the same is true with awe: you may be thunderstruck with the first glimpse of the Grand Canyon, or of a Saturn rocket launching, or of the Queen of England. But the guide who descends daily into the canyon, or the electrician at Cape Kennedy, or the equerry in the palace becomes *accustomed* to the thing. He can't maintain his original awe.

This is as it should be. We have to function. We have to get on with it. T. S. Eliot was right when he said that human kind can't bear very much reality. If we had the whole abyss of mystery and splendor gaping straight at us all the time, we would be paralyzed, or worse, shriveled to a clinker. We would not be able to take it. Tradition used to say that the seraphim, those high and burning celestial lords, could gaze steadily at the Divine Glory; but whether or not they can, we mortals surely cannot.

And so we find, for one thing, that the approaches Heaven has made towards us are "tailored" to our humanity. Sinai was wrapped in thick clouds—and even that proved to be a bit much for everyone. The Shekinah was veiled inside the unapproachable place. And when God himself came to dwell among us, his glory was wrapped in the ordinariness of infant flesh.

But we find that, even with the thing brought low, as it were, our responses are hardly consonant with the immensity of the story. Here is the greatest event of all— God with us—and we do not leap to our feet in a transport of joy. Here is the greatest paradox of all—the Eternal Word incarnate as an infant boy—and we do not boggle.

But if we take our humanness, with its limitations, into account, it is clear that the thing God had in mind when he came to us was not to transfix us, or to mes-merize us into a perpetual trance. It was, rather, by his life of obedience and by his offering up of that life in our behalf, to open up to us again what human life is all about: namely, the liberty to know, love, obey, and worship God in all our appointed tasks. The life he lived here among us, through his infancy, boyhood, adolescence, and young manhood, was, so far as we can tell, a very ordinary one of domesticity, work and play, learning, and obedience to his parents.

That life was a pattern for us, the Scriptures say. And the pattern suggests that, in the ordinary course of events, the thing for us is that we do our work, and learn, slowly perhaps, what it means to live and do that work wholly "unto the Lord." There is one sense in which we can say that the Incarnation raised ordinariness to the possibility of glory. The common life of human flesh was shown to be the very realm in which the Father can be known.

But of course, we were not left with unrelieved ordinariness—a featureless plain, as it were, of sheer, plodding obedience. That would be a daunting vista for the mightiest saint to face. There are peaks—of inspiration, of encouragement, of renewal, and so forth. Or, to change the picture, there is a round, a rhythm. Just as we have the round of the year, with spring, summer, fall, and winter perpetually enacting for us the drama of renewal;

or the round of the month, with the phases of the moon; or of the week, with the one day in seven regularly and rhythmically recurring; or even of the day, with twilight and dawn and the pauses for eating and sleeping organizing our life and work into a solemn dance—just as we have all this in the "natural" course of things, so we may suppose that there is a similar round or rhythm in the spiritual realm.

It is always risky, of course, to separate the natural and the spiritual realms, as though they were two independent worlds. Various religions and cults try it, but no Christian can be satisfied with this dichotomy, holding as he does right at the center of his vision the notion of the Incarnation, that is, that event where the natural became the vehicle for the spiritual, or the eternal was manifest in time.

It is perhaps because of this lively awareness in the Christian vision of the way in which our world and our ordinary life were made the vehicle, or the stage, for the disclosure of the eternal, that the Church has thought it was not amiss to celebrate periodically the great events of the Gospel—Christmas, Epiphany, Lent, Easter, Ascension, and Pentecost—precisely for the renewal and refreshment of the faithful.

Not all the churches in Christendom mark these events, and there is apostolic warrant for either way. St. Paul seems to permit the believers to observe or not to observe, as their outlook inclines them to do. And of course, no one claims that Jesus was born on December 25, or that he rose from the tomb on April 20, say. But it has been a very widespread practice in most of the churches to observe some or all of these occasions, and, if we reflect briefly, we can see how it makes sense.

For one thing, as we have seen, the created order in which we mortal men live is rhythmic, rather than linear and featureless. Spring and fall, dawn and twilight—we have the whole business enacted and vivified for us by earth and sky and trees and living creatures, a sort of natural antiphon, you might say, to some divine pattern. Our eyes and ears and noses are hailed with sights and sounds and smells that recurrently boost us along to renewed awareness of the wonder of this created order.

And, besides this external rhythm, we can find inside our own makeup, as we have seen, this need to be jogged and reminded of what we already know. We have no doubt, for instance, that we are married to our spouse, but the yearly marking of this event seems to spring from something in the very fabric of our being. Or again, we know quite well that our child was *born* one fine day, but we return every year to a formality with candles and cake to mark this event. It is not as though we don't know it. But we need to *enact* it somehow, or to celebrate it.

This, surely, is what the yearly celebration of Christmas suggests for the Christian believer. Here is the recurrent marking and solemnizing of the event that stands above all other events for him— God's appearance in our own flesh, our salvation made nigh, light bursting over our world, life and immortality brought to light, peace declared between God and man. If our own little anniversaries and birthdays claim our recurrent attention, how much more profoundly does the remembrance of this event—which occurred not simply in some legend, or in some transcendent ether, but in our real history— claim our attention.

But there is more. The event celebrated is the supreme point at which our ordinariness was attested to, as it were, by God himself taking our flesh, and our life was raised to glory. So that the things that make up our life here—work and eating and drinking and relationships and music and play and colors and sounds and smells and flavors—become, for the Christian, not simply chance details in a futile grind down toward oblivion but the very forms by which we participate in our appointed realm of the created order.

And so, in one sense, Christmas is the celebration of the birth of our Lord Jesus Christ; but it is more than a mere anniversary of a past event. It is the celebration of our life made new, of our humanness opened out to the possibility of glory; and therefore we bring everything that pertains to that humanness, and we deck this occasion with all of it, affirming that it all "belongs." We call up, in song and pageant and picture and ceremony, the scenes and characters who appeared in that first drama: the Holy Family, Bethlehem, the shepherds, the angels, and the Magi. And we worship and feast and make merry in a hundred ways in honor of it all. We enact, in rituals of gaiety, and of giving and receiving, and of festooning and caroling, the joy that broke upon our world in that little town on that unlikely night.

We bring our wills, like Mary, who said, "Be it unto me according to thy word"; and we bring our adoration, like the shepherds, who hardly knew what they were seeing; and our songs, like the angels; and our offerings, like the Magi. As vividly as we can, we call up these scenes and characters for our imaginations, not by way of charade but in order that our whole being may be roused, by sights and sounds and even tastes and smells—for feasting and incense are of the very stuff of our humanness and have attended joyful occasions and celebrations from time immemorial. And we do this in order that we may find renewed in ourselves the appreciation of the very thing that the Nativity was all about, namely, that the whole of our humanness, and not just our immaterial spirits, is the object of the Divine Love, and the locale of his Incarnation for our salvation.

✵

My Dad's Death Brought Christmas "Home"

Thomas C. Oden

When we got word, my daughter and I were trying to make Christmas trees out of Cheerios. She had made a large pan of green, gooey muck, which (the directions said) we could pour on Cheerios and easily assemble them into little green trees. Soon our hands were so sticky that every time we pulled our fingers away from the tiny trees, the whole tree would collapse or pull apart. Buttering our fingers, we later learned, would have solved the whole problem.

It was in that context that the call came from home that my 85-year-old father had died a peaceful death after a severe illness of about a month.

On the phone were my lawyer brother Tal and my silver-haired, eternally nurturing, inwardly tough 75-year-old mother who had just returned from the hospital. I told them I would be on the first plane home. Within three hours, my wife and I were headed to the airport. As we made our way through the Christmas-clad towns toward the airport, I was filled with a flood of emotions ranging from a deep sense of irretrievable loss, to gratitude and relief that Dad's suffering had not been extended longer.

Above all, I was feeling a deep sense of incongruity between death and Christmas. All about us were signs of Christmas, this most joyous season of birth and celebration, of sparkling decorations and happy carols. Internally I was feeling loss, grief, dissonance, brokenness. This incongruity became a kind of theme that would run all through the week ahead. It is the main reason I am sharing this personal recollection.

Each moment, every sound, smell, and touch, came in an intense relation to the loss I felt. Everything was reflected as if seen through an enormous lens—the lens of my relationship with my dad. A barking dog, a shiny doorknob, the white cloud high in the grey sky, the posture of a middle-aged man, the distant glance of a passerby—all of these fleeting things became magnified in relation to the ache, the memory, the admiration, the trust, the closeness I felt toward my father. I sensed somehow that I would learn something important about myself, about others close to me, about relationships and their meaning, and, perhaps, even of the mysterious movement of providence quietly rearranging the furniture of our lives.

Coming from Newark, New Jersey, to Altus, Oklahoma, from coughing urban sprawl to a small, quiet, southwestern rural town is like moving from one world to another. Instantly I felt the warmth and caring environment of an extended family. The whole town was like an extended family. The marvelous women Mom had known for 40 or 50 years are incredibly resourceful, intelligent, and supportive. I knew I was in a place with a lot of love and determination to do what was necessary for a broken family. It didn't take long for me to realize the importance of visits from old friends, bringing personal affirmation, and displaying social maintenance efforts that would continue long afterward.

Notes came. And not only individuals, but often whole families dropped in briefly, usually bringing food or flowers. These two symbols were outward means of saying, "We're with you, we support you, we love you, we remember your loved one." Sometimes the message was clearer than at others. Often it was simply someone's presence that communicated that he or she cared from the heart.

Another incongruity I began to experience was that when I got home I wanted to be of help to my family. Yet I knew that I myself was so susceptible to instant grief, and wondered if my vulnerability would disturb others.

I reasoned that I must simply be myself, and that if they said, "Tom's having a rough time," it was true, and more likely to elicit the kind of caring response that expresses the deeper solidarity of our family than if I tried to repress my inner pain.

One of the first things I did was to opt out of any officiating function in the funeral. My primary relationship with my father was as a son, not as a minister; I wanted to be with my family. So we talked about how best to pray so as to commend my father to God.

An attorney for over 50 years in the same town, Dad had helped many thousands of people over a long career. But his deepest circle of friendship was among the people of his local church, and among those who shared a broader ministry, concretely expressed in his own small world of Jackson County. His several lifelong interests, which fall roughly into four areas, reveal this: (1) his long-term friendship with blacks, dating from the hazardous days of the Ku Klux Klan to the social problems of the sixties; (2) his work in initiating a ministry to the migrant Mexican-American community; (3) his Indian mission interest as a founding member of a group supportive of the Oklahoma Indian Mission Conference; and (4) his legal efforts to help write legislation and draw up papers for the development of Western Oklahoma State College, a small institution for low-income people who could not go away to expensive residential schools.

All four interests were deeply rooted in a realistic evangelical faith that manifested itself in regular Bible study, daily family prayers at breakfast, and teaching Bible classes for over 50 years. This was the combination, the dialectical energy, that shaped the real interest of his life—evangelical faith and social commitment to the poor. His was a practical, inconspicuous effort to help the needy, such as paying for winter heating bills in the black Methodist church, and trying to get indoor toilets for migrant workers. The same interest was expressed in the religious and temporal life of the Oklahoma Indian, especially in a concern to provide native pastoral leadership for the Oklahoma Indian tribes, and then helping with support. Finally, there was his political action toward developing a small college in our hometown, one anyone could attend.

When friends came by, however, they did not talk about those things. They talked about how Dad had helped them with something at a particular time, how he had shown the love of God in his personal lifestyle. It was on that small, highly personal scale that his life was remembered by each one.

A central vexation emerged in planning the service: the clash of the Christmas symbols and the reality of the funeral, which was planned for December 22. Green armfuls of Christmas hangings were already in place in the sanctuary, and a decorated Christmas tree was in place. Dad had loved Christmas, experienced it as a moment of liturgical fulfillment, of song, of giving, of being together. But I could not quite get my mind around the idea of combining the symbols of the funeral with the symbols of Christmas: they seemed so irreconcilable. I was on the side of keeping the two separated, while others intuitively felt they could somehow go together. Not until we decided on music did some light begin to dawn, for as we selected hymns, it became clear that the hymns Dad most loved were those great ones of the evangelical Protestant tradition. We selected Charles Wesley's "O for a Thousand Tongues to Sing," and John Newton's "Amazing Grace," with its bagpipe chords and simple, powerful words. For the final selection, Mom suggested "Joy to the World," with music by Handel and words by Isaac Watts. Then the light dawned: I knew instantly that was the thing to do, for "Joy to the World," if it were sung as the final act of the congregational praise, would bring integrity and deep meaning to the entire service. So we agreed to leave the Christmas decorations up; we would sing "Joy to the World" at the conclusion of the service of Christian burial. It all seemed right, but at the back of my mind I was still somewhat uneasy about the potential clash of symbolism.

On December 22 I was the first one awake in a house crammed with sleeping guests. I got up as quietly as I could and tried to move about without making a sound, and left as quietly as I could. I had very clearly in my mind what I intended to do: I wanted to walk the eight blocks Dad had walked to work for over 50 years.

My senses seemed extraordinarily sharp on that cool, still, bright December morning. Everything seemed awesomely quiet except for a large number of starlings staking out their territory. I saw a flock of maybe 200 blackbirds against the brightening sky fly from a white picket fence to a long pencil mark of a telephone line. In the distance I could hear some cats fussing, and at a greater distance, sounds of people starting their cars, and the meshing gears of a truck out on the highway.

I was keenly aware of the value of my roots, of my town, my family, my identity. I gave thanks for these unusual gifts in a highly mobile society, and for being able to sustain them even through changes in both my society and me.

It was eight o'clock when I arrived at Lowell's Funeral Home. The door was locked. No one seemed to be stirring. As I turned around, I was surprised to find someone else already waiting: a husky farmer named Ray Ewing, in a Dodge pickup. He greeted me warmly, and spoke openly of his love for Dad and for our whole family. He said, "The world is better for your dad." He left saying he would come back later, and I went back a half-block to the church, where I found the chapel door open. I went in and took the welcome opportunity to meditate and read some Scripture and pray.

In my coat pocket I had an old, leather-bound 1934 Order of Worship. I decided to go through the service of Christian burial and committal by myself, alone and aloud. I was profoundly instructed by each of the prayers. I could not believe how pointed and relevant they could be to me. Step by step I went through that service, realizing this was the best way I could prepare myself. When I finally said aloud, "into thy hands I commend my spirit" (quoting Jesus, an analogy to the committal of the body), I felt a deep sense of completion, of gratitude, and absolute confidence in God's providence, and a personal reassurance that I could move through the day with a sense of affirmation, doing what had to be done.

Returning to the funeral home, I met several friends who had come by to pay their respects to Dad. Each encounter became etched in my memory. Not that what they said was so profound, but that they were there, that they cared.

Many in old age die in nursing homes, more or less alone, with only a handful of people remembering them because they have outlived their contemporaries.

Though Dad outlived almost all his contemporaries, he lived his elder years in vital dialogue with young, growing families, and always had supportive, lively relationships with young people. That is one of the reasons we wanted his pallbearers to come from the family's emerging generation. One of them was my son, whose hair was the longest, and who is deeply immersed in the values of his generation. Yet I can think of no one who had greater affection for Dad. The generations were quietly bridged by his long life, and I sensed in him a sense of futurity as well as history.

I was astonished later when I looked at the list of people who had come to see him. At first I had not paid any attention to the little red-covered record the funeral home keeps of visits, and was not particularly warmed up to the idea of "signing in." Yet by noon on the day of the funeral when I glanced through it, I was amazed to find that the entire book was literally covered with names. There was no more room left! To me, that had a quiet significance: Dad's life was recalled meaningfully by not just his own generation, but by the second and third generations following him in whose growth he delighted.

I had taken along an apple and an orange since I had skipped breakfast, and I ate the apple as I turned from the funeral home and headed back down the street. I had a deep sense of fulfillment; I felt spiritually prepared for the funeral service. But it was not until I had almost reached home that I was hit by the most amazing realization—for me the central spiritual lesson of the entire sequence of events. A very simple thought struck me: *I am the recipient of someone else's goodness.*

I had fantasized: "Suppose I should come back to Altus to live?" Without any merit of my own, I would be an indirect recipient of all the goodness Dad had bestowed upon others.

I suddenly felt I had stumbled upon the center of Christian faith, and with it, the meaning of this entire event.

I wanted to tell somebody, and I hurried home. But it was a busy house that I entered, now only two hours before the funeral. I wanted to greet the many guests arriving from long distances, but I also wanted to find someone with whom I could talk through this insight, which seemed to be the most important thing I had learned for a long time. But I could not find the right moment; the living room became louder and busier. I had to wait for the proper moment to sort out this powerful learning that coalesced all my theological education in a simple awareness: I am the recipient of another's goodness.

In the final moments of the service it all came together, making fitting impact upon my consciousness, and wrapping up the event of my father's passing with great clarity and meaning. It occurred as we stood to sing the last hymn. My eyes were so full of tears I could scarcely read the words, and my voice was quavering so much that I could hardly sing. But we did sing together Isaac Watts's great hymn to Handel's music, "Joy to the World." It, more than anything else, brought together what had seemed to me to be the basic incongruence of the whole week—the tension between Christmas and death, the birth of the Messiah and the death of my father. All of those clashing symbols were unresolved until that moment when we sang, "Joy to the world! the Lord is come; let earth receive her King."

In the last stanza, the meaning of one archaic line— that curious phrase, "far as the curse is found"—finally came through clearly to me. I had sung it many times thinking it was an incomplete sentence, reading "for" for "far." It had seemed so odd and antiquated. But in context, it came through to me that God comes in the Incarnation to make his blessings flow as far as the curse is found, as far as our despair over our own freedom persists, as far as his blessings go. And that is made known in the Incarnation event celebrated at Christmas. That is why "Joy to the World" brought this funeral service to a sense of completion and appropriate fulfillment. I was ready to say, as we did say in the service of Christian burial, "We therefore commit his body to its resting place, but his spirit we commend to God."

✧

Yabba-ka-doodles!

Mike Mason

L ast year, two months before Christmas, I began an "experiment in joy." I decided to be joyful for the next 90 days. Since this was an experiment, there was room for failure.

If at times I felt gloomy, short-tempered, or just plain *blah,* I didn't beat myself up for it. Rather, recognizing that self-condemnation is a chief enemy of joy, I would simply return as best I could to my quiet resolve to rise above all circumstances and do whatever it took to lay hold of joy. In this way, I hoped over the course of 90 days to learn some of joy's secrets and to emerge a more jubilant person. I pictured my joy as a flabby muscle that, if exercised every day, would gradually grow stronger.

The first month of my experiment was amazing. I'm a moody person by nature, and never in my life had I experienced such a steady flow of pure happiness. By the second month, however, difficulties had set in. As Christmas approached, my days were more characterized by struggle than by joy. Still, each day in new and surprising ways, a measure of joy kept coming to me. I was learning not to focus on the darkness but always to look out for the light.

Christmas tends to be a hard time for me, as it is for many. As the angels gather to announce their glad tidings, there is a parallel gathering of the ogres of materialism, busyness, unrealistic expectations, old sadness, and family strife. To be touched by the true joy of Christmas, it seems we must first encounter our own joylessness and our clumsiness at celebration.

In our family we traditionally refer to the day before Christmas Eve as "Christmas Adam." Similarly, the day after Christmas is "Christmas Cain," and the next day is "Christmas Abel." For years we have celebrated Christmas Adam with a story party, a gathering of friends and neighbors who are invited to bring a story or a poem to read aloud. I usually write a short story, someone brings a guitar, and everyone donates goodies. We read and sing and chat and chew, and no finer entertainment can be found anywhere.

This year, however, I'd hardly slept the night before and woke up feeling embroiled in problems. I'm not normally a party person, and the thought of having to get into the holiday mood for a bunch of friends that evening was overwhelming. Worst of all, I was in the middle of a wretched experiment in joy. The happy honeymoon was over. I'd begun to think of joy as a hard taskmistress, and of Christmas as her nasty elder sister.

Fortunately there was one thing that I was looking forward to on Christmas Adam: breakfast with Chris Walton. Chris is that rarest of people, someone who always blesses me. No matter what he's going through, what mood he's in, or what we do together—somehow I always leave his company feeling brushed by heavenly light. As we aren't able to see each other often, our times together are all the more precious.

So, nursing the kind of hangover that comes from imbibing too much gloom, I set off to meet Chris at Ricky's Restaurant for bacon and eggs. Even in times

of tragedy, being with a true friend can have a normal-
izing effect. In Chris's presence, I gradually began to
relax as we talked about favorite books and music, about
Christmas plans, about our families, and about Jesus. I
particularly recall that we discussed, for some reason,
the Jewishness of Jesus and how the only Bible he had
was the Hebrew one. We speculated on what it might
be like to read the Old Testament through Jewish eyes.

The more we talked, the more I sensed a quiet joy tug-
ging at my sleeve like a little child. I cannot say I was
feeling entirely happy by the time we rose to leave, but
a warmth was stealing over me. Still, it was the sort of
thing that might easily have been snatched away by the
next small annoyance, were it not for the strange event
that transpired in the parking lot.

We were standing beside our cars, Chris by his door
and I by mine, saying our goodbyes. Traffic was rushing
by on Fraser Highway, making it difficult to hear. But as
Chris raised his hand in a wave and beamed a last, broad
smile, I distinctly heard him call out, *Yabba-ka-doodles!*

Yabba-what? What did he mean? What language
was this? As we'd just been talking of Jewish matters, I
wondered if Chris might be delivering some traditional
Yiddish holiday greeting. I felt a bit like Mary, who, when

hailed by the angel Gabriel, "wondered what kind of greeting this might be."

"What did you say?" I called back.

This time Chris threw back his head, beamed as brightly as if he were seeing an angel himself, and belted out, *YABBA-KA-DOODLES!*

Chris is not much given to spontaneous ecstatic utterances. Maybe he was just goofing off? More puzzled than ever, I left my car and walked around to where he was standing.

"I don't get it," I said. "Yabba-ka-doodles. What does it mean?"

"Yabba-what?" said Chris.

"*Yabba-ka-doodles.* You said *Yabba-ka-doodles* and I want to know what it means."

"Yabba-ka-doodles? I didn't say Yabba-ka-doodles."

"Then what did you say?"

"I said, 'I'm glad we could do this.' "

"I'm glad we could do this?" I echoed blankly.

For a moment we stared at one another, listening to the sound of this inane, colorless sentence against the rapturous syllables of Yabba-ka-doodles.

And then we both burst into laughter, wild, hilarious, thigh-slapping gales of it there in Ricky's parking lot. It was so absurd a mistake, so gloriously unlikely. And partly because of that, it filled us with that unlikeliest of qualities in this darkly unsettling world—joy! It was a rich and preposterous joy, as surprising as if Santa Claus himself (or his Yiddish uncle) had come thundering down out of the sky in his sleigh.

All the way home in the car I kept muttering, caressing, shouting that silly word—*"Yabba-ka-doodles ... Yabba-ka-doodles"*—giggling and guffawing like a schoolboy. Talk about joy! More than happy, I felt drunk with joy for the rest of that day. And when Chris and I saw each other next, on Christmas Eve, we nearly jumped into each other's arms, yelling, *"Yabba-ka-doodles,* brother!"

Who would have believed that so much joy could be contained in one crazy, purely imagined word? Later I wondered: Were my ears playing tricks, or is it possible that Chris, without realizing it, really did say *Yabba-ka-doodles?* Was he unknowingly used as a messenger of God to me, delivering the joyous news of Christmas in an angelic tongue?

When I was a student at Regent College, one of my Old Testament professors was Bruce Waltke, who had worked on the translation committee for the New International Version. In his lectures, Dr. Waltke loved to linger over the subtleties of ancient Hebrew, expounding different interpretations of a single word or phrase, and building a strong case for his own favored translation. Yet he also pointed out that translation is not salvation. As he was fond of saying, "I've known people who were saved through a verse of Scripture that I know is mistranslated."

On Christmas Adam last year, I was transported into joy through a phrase I had misunderstood, which has now entered my vocabulary as a traditional Christmas greeting. And so, as Tiny Tim piped up, "God bless us, every one," I say resoundingly to each and every one of you: *Yabba-ka-doodles!*

✧

The Advent of Humility

Tim Keller

Innumerable Christmas devotionals point out the humble circumstances of Jesus' birth—among shepherds, in a crude stable, with a feed trough for a bassinet. When Jesus himself tried to summarize why people should take up the yoke of following him, he said it was because he was meek and humble (Matt 11:29). Seldom, however, do we explore the full implications of how Jesus' radical humility shapes the way we live our lives every day.

Humility is crucial for Christians. We can only receive Christ through meekness and humility (Matt 5:3, 5; 18:3–4). Jesus humbled himself and was exalted by God

(Phil 2:8–9); therefore joy and power through humility is the very dynamic of the Christian life (Luke 14:11; 18:14; 1 Pet 5:5).

The teaching seems simple and obvious. The problem is that it takes great humility to understand humility, and even more to resist the pride that comes so naturally with even a discussion of the subject.

We are on slippery ground because humility cannot be attained directly. Once we become aware of the poison of pride, we begin to notice it all around us. We hear it in the sarcastic, snarky voices in newspaper columns and weblogs. We see it in civic, cultural, and business leaders who never admit weakness or failure. We see it in our neighbors and some friends with their jealousy, self-pity, and boasting.

And so we vow not to talk or act like that. If we then notice "a humble turn of mind" in ourselves, we immediately become smug—but that is pride in our humility. If we catch ourselves doing *that* we will be particularly impressed with how nuanced and subtle we have become.

Humility is so shy. If you begin talking about it, it leaves. To even ask the question, "Am I humble?" is to not be so. Examining your own heart, even for pride, often leads to being proud about your diligence and circumspection.

Christian humility is not thinking less of yourself; it is thinking of yourself less, as C. S. Lewis so memorably said. It is to be no longer always noticing yourself and how you are doing and how you are being treated. It is "blessed self-forgetfulness."

Humility is a byproduct of belief in the gospel of Christ. In the gospel, we have a confidence not based in our performance but in the love of God in Christ (Rom 3:22–24). This frees us from having to always be looking at ourselves. Our sin was so great, nothing less than the death of Jesus could save us. He *had* to die for us. But his love for us was so great, Jesus was *glad* to die for us.

We are on slippery ground when we discuss humility, because religion and morality inhibit humility. It is common in the evangelical community to talk about one's worldview—a set of basic beliefs and commitments that shape the way we live in every particular. Others prefer the term "narrative identity." This is a set of answers to the questions, "Who am I? What is my life all about? What am I here for? What are the main barriers keeping me from fulfillment? How can I deal with those barriers?"

There are two basic narrative identities at work among professing Christians. The first is what I will call the moral-performance narrative identity. These are people who in their heart of hearts say, *I obey; therefore I am accepted by God.* The second is what I will call the grace narrative identity. This basic operating principle is, *I am accepted by God through Christ; therefore I obey.*

People living their lives on the basis of these two different principles may superficially look alike. They may sit right beside one another in the church pew, both striving to obey the law of God, to pray, to give money generously, to be good family members. But they are doing so out of radically different motives, in radically different spirits, resulting in radically different personal characters.

When persons living in the moral-performance narrative are criticized, they are furious or devastated because they cannot tolerate threats to their self-image of being a "good person."

But in the gospel our identity is not built on such an image, and we have the emotional ballast to handle criticism without attacking back. When people living in the moral-performance narrative base their self-worth on being hard working or theologically sound, then they *must* look down on those whom they perceive to be lazy or theologically weak.

But those who understand the gospel cannot possibly look down on anyone, since they were saved by sheer grace, not by their perfect doctrine or strong moral character.

Another mark of the moral-performance narrative is a constant need to find fault, win arguments, and prove that all opponents are not just mistaken but dishonest sellouts. However, when the gospel is deeply grasped, our need to win arguments is removed, and our language becomes gracious. We don't have to ridicule our opponents, but instead we can engage them respectfully.

People who live in the moral-performance narrative use sarcastic, self-righteous put-down humor, or have no sense of humor at all. Lewis speaks of "the unsmiling concentration upon Self, which is the mark of hell." The gospel, however, creates a gentle sense of irony. We find a lot to laugh at, starting with our own weaknesses. They don't threaten us anymore because our ultimate worth is not based on our record or performance.

Martin Luther had the basic insight that moralism is the default mode of the human heart. Even Christians who believe the gospel of grace on one level can continue to operate as if they have been saved by their works. In "The Great Sin" in *Mere Christianity,* Lewis writes, "If we find that our religious life is making us feel that we are good—above all, that we are better than someone else—I think we may be sure that we are being acted on, not by God, but by the Devil."

Gracious, self-forgetful humility should be one of the primary things that distinguishes Christian believers from the many other types of moral, decent people in the world. But I think it is fair to say that humility, which is a key differentiating mark of the Christian, is largely missing in the church. Nonbelievers, detecting the stench of sanctimony, turn away.

Some will say, "Phariseeism and moralism are not our culture's big problems right now. Our problems are license and antinomianism. There is no need to talk about grace all the time to postmodern people." But postmodern people have been rejecting Christianity for years, thinking that it was indistinguishable from moralism. Only if you show them there's a difference—that what they rejected wasn't real Christianity—will they even begin to listen again.

This is the place where the author is supposed to come up with practical solutions. I don't have any. Here's why.

First, the problem is too big for practical solutions. The wing of the evangelical church that is most concerned about the loss of truth and about compromise is actually infamous in our culture for its self-righteousness and pride. However, there are many in our circles who, in reaction to what they perceive as arrogance, are backing away from many of the classic Protestant doctrines (such as Forensic Justification and Substitutionary Atonement) that are crucial and irreplaceable—as well as the best possible resources for humility.

Second, directly talking about practical ways to become humble, either as individuals or as communities, will always backfire. I have said that major wings of the evangelical church are wrong. So who is left? Me? Am I beginning to think only we few, we happy few, have achieved the balance that the church so needs? I think I hear Wormwood whispering in my ear, "Yes, only you can really see things clearly."

I do hope to clarify, or I wouldn't have written on the topic at all. But there is no way to begin telling people how to become humble without destroying what fragments of humility they may already possess.

Third, humility is only achieved as a byproduct of understanding, believing, and marveling in the gospel of grace. But the gospel doesn't change us in a mechanical way. Recently I heard a sociologist say that for the most part, the frameworks of meaning by which we navigate our lives are so deeply embedded in us that they operate "pre-reflectively." They don't exist only as a list of propositions, but also as themes, motives, and attitudes. When we listen to the gospel preached or meditate on it in the Scriptures, we are driving it so deeply into our hearts, imaginations, and thinking that we begin to instinctively "live out" the gospel.

So let us preach grace till humility just starts to grow in us.

✵

The Wondrous Gift

Elisabeth Elliot

It was not to the throne room of a king, where he would have been received in solemn majesty, that he came that night. It was not to the banqueting hall of a governor with its flickering torches, its loaded tables, and its throng of revelers, nor to the packed inn where frantic serving maids ran in and out, answering the surly cries of hungry travelers. It was to starlit fields, where in silence broken only by the soft sounds of sleeping sheep the shepherds were doing what they were supposed to be doing, that he came—the angel of the Lord, in the terrifying glory of the Lord, bringing with him the good news of a great joy for all people, even for them, the shepherds.

We are told that they went as fast as they could to Bethlehem to see what had happened. They found the Savior of the world with Mary and Joseph, though how they found him we are not told, nor how they recognized him as Christ the Lord there in the dark cave, in the animals' manger. We are told that they reported what the angel had said to them and then went back to their fields. That is all that we know they did, but we imagine more. We see them kneeling in the straw, offering to the baby their worship and, perhaps, some simple gift. We imagine everyone who came kneeling down in adoration, humble and glad in the steamy darkness, laying before the Child some present. A twelfth-century Christian pictured even the animals bringing their gifts:

> I, said the donkey, all shaggy and brown,
> I carried His mother uphill and down.
> I carried His mother to Bethlehem town.
> I, said the donkey, all shaggy and brown.
>
> I, said the cow, all white and red,
> I gave Him my manger for a bed.
> I gave Him my hay to pillow His head.
> I, said the cow, all white and red.

I, said the sheep, with curly horn,

I gave Him my wool for a blanket warm.

He wore my coat on Christmas morn.

I, said the sheep, with curly horn.

So every beast, by some good spell,

In the stable rude was glad to tell

Of the gift he gave Immanuel,

The gift he gave Immanuel.

We cannot imagine adoration without gift-giving, and at Christmas we have the opportunity, by wise and honored custom, of expressing appreciation and love to others by making them presents.

We offer to God our thanksgiving for his "unspeakable gift," that little child at whose birth angels sang, a human being, coming into the human scene for the sake of humans—all of us, the shepherds, the mysterious sages from the East, godly Jews who had looked all their lives long for the Messiah, all the rest of the teeming world. "Joy which shall be to all people." We think of that gift, and we thank him.

We think of God's other gifts and most of us wonder, at Christmas time, what gift we may give to him beyond our thanksgiving. Money, time, talent, possessions? We check them off impatiently. "I do tithe, I give my time, I share what I have." Or perhaps we check off the list with diffidence, asking, "Of what use will that be for God?"

Yet we know that all we have is given to us by God. "Every good gift and every perfect gift is from above, and cometh down from the Father of Lights." So we give him back a portion of what was always his, trusting him to accept it and make use of it in his own way. It is not beyond our powers to imagine God's making of our time, money, talents, and possessions instruments of good in the world.

But there is one other thing we may offer, something that seems perhaps much more our own, of much less "use" to the world at large, and a paltry present at best, one we are sometimes hesitant to surrender. Christina Rosetti's lovely carol reminds us of it:

> What can I give Him, poor as I am?
> If I were a shepherd, I would bring a lamb.
> If I were a wise man, I would do my part.
> What can I give Him—give my heart.

How am I to do this? Some measure of trust and commitment is involved in the giving of any gift. The child proffers the crushed dandelion to his mother, sure that she can be trusted to be pleased with it and—what matters far more to him—to receive him. It is not to obtain the mother's love that the child gives her the flower, but because he knows he has already obtained it. To lay my heart before Christ the Lord would be unthinkable without the same confidence felt by the child—the assurance of acceptance, not that I may hope to receive grace but that grace has already been poured upon me. In all my giving I only appropriate God's supreme gift.

I bring, then, my heart—all my heart—an unopened parcel. No one else knows what it contains, but I myself know there is nothing there of gold, frankincense, or myrrh. There is nothing in the parcel except the panic, the fear, the chaos of whatever storm buffets me now, and, like the disciples in a storm-tossed boat, I find, to my amazement, that I am given something in return—peace, the peace of God that passes understanding.

I bring, like the five thousand long ago, my hunger, and like them I am fed.

I bring the darkness of my heart, even that worst darkness which prefers darkness, and, simply because I have brought it, the Light that no darkness can comprehend shines in.

It may be that the heart I have to offer is a broken one. If so, I bring a broken heart. And somehow, after a time, I receive healing.

I bring whatever there may be of ashes, mourning, the spirit of heaviness, and I go away with beauty, with the oil of joy, with the garment of praise.

The story is told of a hermit who, having suffered the loss of all things in his renunciation of the world, yet found no peace. It seemed to him in his lonely cell that the Lord was asking something more.

"But I have given you everything!" cried the hermit.

"All but one thing," answered the Lord.

"What is it, Lord?"

"Your sins."

Like the hermit, I bring also my sins, for they, too, are contained in the parcel. And I receive in exchange forgiveness.

It is a tremendous mystery—out of this darkness, this song; out of this chaos, this peace, Christ giving to us himself. And we, in mysterious exchange for the crushed dandelion that would have been of no use to anyone at all, are granted precious things that, even more inexplicably, we may give in turn to other people. We may participate, through this transformation, in the work of the

Prince of Peace in the world, giving away joy and peace, things listed in no Christmas catalogue. It may well be that some of the gifts we had sighed over in the catalogue were withheld precisely in order that we might receive instead priceless ones for the sake of others, gifts whose sharing, far from impoverishing, enriches the giver.

> How silently, how silently, the wondrous gift is
> given.
> So God imparts to human hearts the blessings of
> His heaven.
> No ear may hear His coming, yet in this world of
> sin
> Where meek souls will receive Him still the dear
> Christ enters in.

✶

The Most Beautiful Story Ever Told

Frank E. Gaebelein

No Christian festival is celebrated more widely and often more superficially outside as well as inside the church than Christmas. As the observance of the birth of Jesus Christ, Christmas stands at the heart of the story of redemption that is uniquely unfolded in the Bible. Here in the event of the Nativity is the center of human history. Of all who have ever lived, none is closer to human life and destiny than Christ. If "the hinge of history is Jesus Christ," as Charles Malik has said, it is because of what happened at Bethlehem nearly 2,000 years ago when the living God invaded human history through the Incarnation.

The celebration of Christmas came comparatively late in church history—not, in fact, until the fourth century. The word "Christmas" does not appear in the Bible, although the Jewish December festival, Hanukkah, is mentioned in the New Testament: "Then came the Feast of Dedication" (John 10:22 NIV).

Not only is there no biblical mention of the word Christmas, but the Bible gives us no mandate for celebrating Jesus' birth, as it does for the sacraments or ordinances of the Lord's Supper and baptism, which by Christ's own command were observed from the very beginning of the church.

Celebration of the other great festivals of the church—Easter with its joyful celebration of the resurrection preceded by Good Friday with its moving remembrance of the crucifixion, and the Feast of Pentecost with its celebration of the descent of the Holy Spirit on the infant church—while also not prescribed in the New Testament, goes back much further than the Festival of Christmas, perhaps to the end of the first century or the beginning of the second.

To trace the origins of Christmas as the Festival of the Nativity, as it is defined by The Oxford English Dictionary, is an exercise in early church history. Scholars, in fact, are by no means agreed on the details of how it developed. The earliest reference to December 25 as the date for the Nativity occurs in the Philocalian calendar, which refers to its Roman observance in AD 336. But recognition of December 25 had been preceded by that of another date—January 6, when Epiphany was celebrated—first in relation to the baptism of Jesus in the river Jordan and later in relation to the coming of the wise men, or Magi, to worship the infant Jesus. By the end of the fourth century there is evidence of the widespread celebration of Jesus' birth on December 25. For example, Chrysostom, in a sermon preached at Antioch about AD 386, said that the feast on December 25 was known from Thrace to Cadiz. But though December 25 has found uniform acceptance—except in the Armenian Church, which celebrates the Nativity on January 6—it is, of course, only the traditional date. We have no real evidence for the exact month and day of Jesus' birth. Nor can we be completely certain of its year. Yet good evidence brings us close to the actual date, which was probably 4 or 5 BC (though some scholars say 7 or 8 BC).

That the Christmas festival had certain pagan relation-
ships is well known. One of the great festivals of ancient
Rome was related to the winter solstice, celebrated on
December 25 as the Natal Day of the Unconquerable
Sun and tied to the Persian religion of Mithraism, one of
Christianity's early rivals. The church took over this day
to turn the attention of Christians from the old heathen
festival to the celebration of the "sun of righteousness."

Likewise, many of our cherished Christian customs
have non-Christian origins. The merriment and giving
of gifts, especially to children, may reflect the Roman
Saturnalia, celebrated from December 17 to 24. As for
the use of greenery and lights, this goes back to the celebration of the Kalends of January in ancient Rome.
The Yule customs have ancient Germano-Celtic back-
grounds. Many European countries have contributed to
the Christmas observance. The crèche came from Italy;
the Christmas tree originated in Germany in the late six-
teenth century and was established in England early in
the nineteenth century by Prince Albert; we are indebted
to Holland for Santa Claus.

Because of the extrabiblical origins of certain aspects
of the Christmas festival, some Christians in the past
have suppressed its celebration. During Cromwell's

time in seventeenth-century England it was banned by Parliament, and in old New England the celebration of Christmas was officially forbidden.

Few Christians today, however, even among the most conservative groups, would go to these lengths. Many of our happy Christmas customs have long since lost their pagan connotations; perhaps it is through God's common grace that they have found a place in the celebration of Christ's birth. As for the present-day commercialization of this beloved festival, typified by the endless repetition of Christmas carols in shopping centers with scarcely a thought for the meaning of their words, this is not celebration; it is desecration!

Christmas is like a many-faceted jewel, and surely one of its loveliest facets is the way it has enriched music and the arts and literature. The distinguished music critic, Paul Hume, said of a Christmas performance in Washington Cathedral of Benjamin Britten's "A Boy Is Born": "One of the wonderful things regarding this time of year is that there is an endless treasure of beautiful music for it, touching all moods and telling the central story in many different ways." Indeed, if Christ had never been born, culture would have been immeasurably impoverished. Have you ever looked at a painting like Raphael's "Alba Madonna," or read a poem like Milton's "Ode on the Nativity," or heard Handel's *Messiah*, and thought, "This would never have been had Christ not been born"?

But turn from the facets to the jewel itself, that authentic historical event of the Nativity. Here we must go back to the first chapter of Matthew's Gospel and the first two chapters of Luke's Gospel, the source documents for the events on which Christmas depends. They are, first of all, authentic historical documents. New Testament scholarship has traveled a long way since the early nineteenth century, when F. C. Baur and the Tübingen critics in Germany denied the authenticity of most of the New Testament. A few years ago W. F. Albright of Johns Hopkins University declared that the whole of the New Testament was written between AD 40–80. And more recently the Cambridge scholar J. A. T. Robinson has argued that all of the New Testament books must be dated before AD 70.

Despite their many differences, the opening chapters of Matthew and Luke have these things in common: that Jesus was born in Bethlehem of a virgin named Mary; that Mary was betrothed to a man named Joseph, who was of the Davidic line; that Jesus' conception by the Holy Spirit was supernaturally announced; that the child who was born was the Christ, the promised Messiah, for the Greek *christos* from which we get the word "Christ" is the equivalent of the Hebrew "Messiah," to whose coming the Old Testament points; and finally, that the child born at Bethlehem was the Savior.

But what about the variations between these two accounts of the Christmas event? It is Matthew who tells us most about Mary's betrothed husband, Joseph. It is in Matthew's Gospel that we read the story of the Magi and the guiding star that has long fascinated astronomers and been the subject of Christmas displays in various planetariums. It is Matthew who also tells us of King Herod's desire to kill the infant Jesus.

As for Luke, we owe to him our knowledge of the angel Gabriel's annunciation to Mary that she would be the virgin mother of Jesus. Luke tells us of the census that took Joseph and Mary from Nazareth to Bethlehem. We learn also from him of the crowded inn and the manger where the baby was laid, and through him we hear the angels' song: "Glory to God in the highest and on earth peace, good will toward men."

The two accounts do not contradict, but comple-
ment each other. Taken together they give us in words
of restraint and simplicity that go straight to our hearts
the most beautiful story ever told.

Moreover, no one can read these narratives carefully without recognizing how Jewish they are. Matthew
begins with a genealogy. He sees Christ's birth as the
fulfillment of Old Testament prophecy in Isaiah, Micah,
Hosea, and Jeremiah. He reports that the child was to
be called Jesus—the Greek form of the Hebrew name
Joshua, meaning "The LORD (Yahweh) is salvation," and
also identifies him with the prophetic name "Immanuel,"
meaning "God with us."

In a different but no less unmistakable way Luke's
account of the Nativity is steeped in the Old Testament.
He begins with the birth of John the Baptist to Zacharias,
a priest in the temple at Jerusalem, and with his wife
Elizabeth, a relative of Mary. After the annunciation, Mary visits Elizabeth, who honors her as the
mother-to-be of the Messiah. So Luke gives us Mary's
wonderful song of praise, the Magnificat, so reminiscent
of Hannah's song before the birth of Samuel. Again, it is
from Luke that we know that Jesus was circumcised in

the temple and later presented there with his mother in obedience to the law of Moses.

This Hebrew matrix of Nativity narratives shows the integral relation of the Christmas event to the whole of biblical history. This most marvelous of happenings when, as Christians have always believed, the living God himself entered human life, takes us to the heart of the biblical view of history. This is not a cyclical view but a linear one, moving forward to an end. Above all, the Bible is the revealed record of God's redemptive work in history, culminating in the life, death, resurrection, and coming again of the Christ who was born in Bethlehem.

Like all the events in redemption history, the Christmas event is both particular and universal. He who was born on the first Christmas day is more than a denominational figure. He is too great to be the exclusive possession of any church or any theology. In his universal significance he is greater than any creed, important though creeds are.

What, then, is Christmas really about? What does it say to us in 1979? Such questions have many answers, and your answer and mine inevitably reflect who we are at the deepest level of our being. But allow me to answer them briefly out of my convictions as you must answer them out of yours.

Christmas shows us the supreme expression of love—the love of God himself who cared enough for us and all mankind to enter into human life in his one and only Son, Jesus Christ. For, as Paul said: "God was in Christ, reconciling the world unto himself." Once we grasp the greatness of God's self-giving love, then, Christmas tells us, we must love others as God has loved us.

John said it with beautiful simplicity in his first epistle:

"Dear friends, let us love one another, for love comes from God. Everyone who loves has been born of God and knows God. Whoever does not love does not know God, because God is love. This is how God showed his love among us; He sent his one and only Son into the world that we might live through him. This is love: not that we loved God, but that he loved us and sent his Son as an atoning sacrifice for our sins. Dear friends, since God so loved us, we also ought to love one another" (1 John 4:7–11 NIV).

The warmth and joy and peace of Christmas must be shared, not hugged to ourselves. For the world today, with all its turmoil and tragedy, Christmas is the eloquent reminder that God has not given up on humanity. It is the enduring assurance that he is involved in our affairs, that he really does enter into our human life and history through his own dear Son.

✦

Our Divine Distortion

Carolyn Arends

When I found a brand new laptop for half price on eBay, I told my friend and musical colleague Spencer about my bargain of a find. He was worried: "Usually when something's too good to be true ..."

"I know," I replied impatiently, "but the seller has a 100 percent approval rating."

"Be careful," warned Spencer.

"Of course," I assured him, annoyed. I wasn't born yesterday.

I sent the seller $1,300 and discovered in very short, sickening order that I had fallen prey to a classic scam.

A fraudster had hacked someone's eBay identity in order to relieve easy marks like me of our money.

I felt an absolute fool—and didn't want to tell Spencer. The next time I saw his number on my caller ID, I didn't answer. I could just imagine his "I told you so."

Soon, I was avoiding Spencer completely. And I started to resent him. Why did he have to be so judgmental? Why couldn't he be on my side? Why was I ever friends with that jerk?

Eventually, we had to fly together to perform at a concert. "Whatever happened with that computer thing?" he asked an hour into the flight. Cornered, I finally confessed my foolishness, dreading the inevitable response. But as soon as I told Spencer about my mistake, a strange thing happened. The enemy I had turned him into evaporated. Spencer turned into Spencer again, my teasing but deeply empathetic buddy.

As embarrassed as I was by my eBay error, I felt even dumber about the way I had allowed my shame to distort my perception of a best friend. If my hand had not been forced, I would have remained estranged from him indefinitely.

I've always considered myself perceptive, but the longer I live, the more I discover my susceptibility to misinterpretation. This is true of the way I view my friends, truer of the way I see my enemies, and perhaps truest of the way I perceive God.

I was raised to understand that sin's gravest consequence is the way it forces God to perceive me: God is holy, I'm not, and there's no way he can even look at me until I have the covering of Christ's blood. In my teens, I clipped a poem out of a youth magazine in which the poet asks—and answers—a pressing question: "How can a righteous God look at me, a sinner, and see a precious child? Simple: The Son gets in his eyes."

But what about how I look at God? I've often been oblivious to one of the most insidious byproducts of the Fall: Sin affects my perception of God. Or, to turn a phrase from that poem, the sin gets in my eyes.

Before Adam and Eve had fallen for the first lie, they basked in God's company. But after a few bites of forbidden fruit, they no longer looked forward to seeing their Maker. When he came calling, they hid.

Had God changed? No. Adam and Eve's brokenness altered their perception of God, not his character. Ever since, we humans have been letting our shame poison our understanding of God. He becomes an ogre, or a bookkeeper, or maybe just a disinterested, detached monarch.

Many of us unconsciously relate to God our Father as a Godfather—there's a lot he can do for us when he likes us, but don't get on his bad side. So we avoid him. And the longer we refuse to take his calls, the worse the distortion becomes.

But here is some good news: Jesus is the antidote to our misperceptions. When we speak of the Incarnation, we acknowledge that Jesus is "God con carne"—God with meat on. Our questions about God's character—Is he really about mercy, justice, and a love that just won't quit?—are answered in the person of Jesus.

In one sense, Adam and Eve were right to fear facing God. The consequences of their choices were painful. But even God's seemingly harshest judgment—banishment from the Garden and the Tree of Life—was rooted in love. If the first humans had accessed eternal life in Eden, they would have remained in their brokenness forever. God chose another way—a death and resurrection way that would cost him much—because he was and is and always will be with us and for us.

Christmas clarifies this resoundingly. That's why every time the angels announced Christ's birth they said, "Do not be afraid." Yes, we should fear sin's consequences.

But we need not fear the perfect love of a God willing to come and shiver in our skin to save us.

We do not have the power to change God's character. Our Father is our Father. Always has been, always will be. But we will never see him for who he really is until the Son gets in our eyes.

Mary Rejoicing, Rachel Weeping

Wendy Murray Zoba

In Honduras, where I used to live, people celebrate *el dia de los inocentes* ("Day of the Innocents") on December 28, "commemorating" the children who were slaughtered in Bethlehem after Jesus was born. It is much like our April Fools' day; people play practical jokes, and those who fall for them are *los inocentes*, which struck me as a strange way to remember this tragedy. But, intended or not, there is a shrewd logic beneath this contradiction.

The disastrous event that took place in Bethlehem when Herod ordered the slaughter of all the boys two years old and under is part of the picture of Christmas, too. But we tend to allow sleigh bells, evergreens, and shopping frenzies to push it out of view. Yet it is, in fact, in all its brutality, what Christmas is about: the Savior's "invasion" (to borrow from C. S. Lewis) and his confrontation with the forces of evil. To subsume this aspect in wafts of potpourri and roasting chestnuts misses the essence of Christmas and sets us up—like the Hondurans who fall for the practical jokes—as the innocent fools.

Matthew's narrative of Christ's birth juxtaposes noble and wretched characters in stark contrasts: stars and swords; majestic kingly visitations and twisted kingly agitation; Mary rejoicing, Rachel weeping; the children who die, and the Child who gets away. How do we reconcile the glorious birth of our Savior with the bloody death of those boys?

There is no extrabiblical documentation of Herod's heinous act. But Bethlehem was truly a "little town" (with a population of between 300 and 1,000, according to some commentators). So it is within the bounds of possibility that the deaths of a few children ("perhaps a dozen or so," according to D. A. Carson) were overshadowed by the many other atrocities Herod committed during his turbulent, twisted reign.

The Magi were not kings and may not have been three, but were, in any case, wise. Skilled astronomers and members of a priestly caste who may have been Zoroastrian, they were industrious, courageous, and truth-seeking pagans from present-day Iran or thereabouts.

One biblical historian suggests that they left Persia late in 3 BC, after Jesus was born, and arrived in late 2 BC, when Jesus was a toddler. By the time they found the child, his family was ensconced in a "house" (Matt 2:10), and Herod calculated that the child could have been born up to two years earlier.

Herod, in the meantime, suffered from "distemper," which the historian Josephus said "greatly increased upon him after a severe manner." "His bowels were also ulcerated" and he had "a difficulty of breathing, which was very loathsome, on account of the stench of his breath." All this topped off his well-attested paranoiac ravings, which had already driven him to command that his wife (whom he dearly loved), along with his two promising sons, be executed. This man "of great barbarity towards all men equally" had been confirmed "King of the Jews" in 40 BC by the Roman senate. Little wonder, then, that at this decrepit stage of life he was in no mood to hear word of one "born king of the Jews."

Were it not for a faith rooted in things unseen, we are tempted to conclude that during this savage episode in God's saving activity his "controlling hand" must have been temporarily stayed. What does one say to the mothers of those boys? Their deaths made no sense: What did they have to do with earthly thrones and messianic expectations?

Matthew calls on the ghost of Rachel, as portrayed by the prophet Jeremiah in his lament for the deported descendants of Israel, to express the grief of these mothers:

> A cry of anguish is heard in Ramah—
> and weeping unrestrained.
> Rachel weeps for her children,
> refusing to be comforted—
> for her children are dead. (Jer 31:15 NLT)

A mother weeping for her lost children is as bad as it gets in this life. It is God's chosen metaphor for the apogee of anguish. Ramah was where the Jews gathered before they were carried off to Babylon. There, Rachel's weeping gives voice to God's own lament over the loss of his children. Rachel herself died in sorrow as she gave birth to her second son, naming him Ben-Oni ("son of my trouble"); she died "on the way" (to Bethlehem), never securing a permanent home. Rachel was not comforted.

But Rachel's anguish serves also as a metaphor for mothers everywhere who face tragic circumstances related to their children. I've read about a mother in America who combed drug-infested streets in search of her wayward offspring and of mothers in Africa who risk all to redeem their kidnapped and enslaved sons. There are mothers everywhere whose tidy worlds are shattered by unexpected tragedy, as Vickilynn Haycraft's was when her three-year-old son, Benjamin, died suddenly while playing on a playground because of a genetic disorder. She wrote a poem:

> How can I pray
> all that's in my heart
> Did You turn away?
> You let my boy die
> You could have healed
> I never said good-bye

Rachel's anguish was near to me, too, when my sister's two-year-old daughter fell ten feet from a window and should have escaped with a broken arm but, instead, died. I asked why Jesus would heal Jairus's daughter when her father pled for her life but didn't heal my niece. Surely her parents' pleas were no less heartfelt.

Ivan Karamazov, who for Feodor Dostoyevsky represents the intellectual agnostic, poses a question to his spiritually sensitive brother, Alyosha: "But then, what about the children? How will we ever account for their sufferings?"

Ivan acknowledges a kind of justice for humans who have made bad choices and suffer, and even for the suffering attendant to the general rebellion of the human race: These thinking adults "have eaten from their apple of knowledge; they know about good and evil and are gods themselves. And they keep eating the apple." But, he says, "little children haven't eaten it."

"Those tears [of children who suffer] must be atoned for. ... How is it possible to atone for them?" he asks. "If the suffering of little children is needed to complete the sum total of suffering required to pay for the truth, I don't want that truth, and I declare in advance that all the truth in the world is not worth the price."

"We cannot afford to pay so much for a ticket," he says. "And so I hasten to return the ticket I've been sent. ... It isn't that I reject God; I am simply returning him most respectfully the ticket that would entitle me to a seat."

Perhaps if the mothers of Bethlehem understood that the birth of the Savior would cost them the lives of their sons, they might have returned their tickets, too. Had they also known of the dream that alerted Joseph to flee, they might have asked, "What harm would there have been in God sending us dreams, too?"

I am not pretending to answer that question. Even Dostoyevsky admitted that when he wrote his dialogue between Ivan and Alyosha he wasn't sure he would be able to answer Ivan's question. But that is not to say there is no hope of illumination by exploring it.

It could be argued—in a twisted way—that it might have been more "just" if Joseph and Mary's son had perished with the rest of the boys. The aching question would not have remained: Why did God save him and not all? But gospel logic asserts that in saving the One, God did save them all. In fact, the One who got away is the ticket that Ivan so cavalierly handed back to God.

Jesus had to get away in order to face the day when the angels would not intervene and when Joseph would not whisk him to Egypt; when Mary, not Rachel, wept and could not be comforted. Jesus "got away" so that he could later on "atone for" the blood of those children and their mothers' tears.

In *The Lord and His Prayer*, N. T. Wright says that in "the prayer for Deliverance from Evil the dominant image ... is that of the Waiting Mother." When Jesus delivered us from evil, he went, like the mothers I read about, to crime-ridden streets and bought back his loved ones from slavery. He answered Vickilynn Haycraft's question, "Did you turn away?" No, he went, Wright writes, "solo and unaided into the whirlpool [of evil], so that it may exhaust its force on him and let the rest of the world go free." Jesus, in the end, was the one "who was not delivered from evil."

In the verse that follows Rachel's lament, Jeremiah writes: "Do not weep any longer, for I will reward you. Your children will come back to you." God's portrait of grief—the weeping mother—is painted over with his picture of joy and resolution: children returning! The prophet Isaiah describes it:

See, I will give a signal to the godless
nations. They will carry your little sons
back to you in their arms; they will bring
your daughters on their shoulders. (Isa 49:22 NLT)
So Rachel will be comforted after all.

Dostoyevsky probed Ivan's question through the godly Father Zossima, who comforts a grieving mother: "Don't you know how bold these little ones are before the throne of the Lord? ... Weep, but every time you do, remember that your little son is ... looking down on you from where he is now, that he sees and rejoices in your tears and shows them to God."

"You will shed a mother's tears for a long time to come," he says, "but in the end your weeping will turn into quiet joy."

When we sing about Bethlehem, we can overlook the phrase that says that "hopes and fears" came together there. Christmas is not "mere good cheer," Wright says. For all the twists in the Christmas narrative, and for all its crushing contrasts, it ultimately is "when darkness breaks ... with the human cry of a small baby, blinking up at his Mother in the sudden light, and seeing her face."

✴

Simeon and the Child Jesus

Harold John Ockenga

"Then took he him up in his arms, and blessed God, and said, Lord, now lettest thou thy servant depart in peace" (Luke 2:28, 29).[7] In this beautiful scene, the aged Simeon takes the baby Jesus up in his arms and expresses his delight and joy to God in a brief prayer. We often picture Jesus taking little children in his arms, and we sing, "I would like to have been with him then," but this thought of another receiving Jesus into his arms is much less familiar to us.

---

7. Scripture quotations in this article are from the King James Version.

The event occurred when Joseph and Mary brought the child to the temple to present him to the Lord, according to the law of Moses. The holy family had made its little pilgrimage from Bethlehem to Jerusalem, a distance of about five miles, to accomplish what was called the purification of Mary. This required the presentation of a lamb, or for those who were poor, of two pigeons. In addition, a gift of five shekels to the temple was required as an acknowledgment of God's claim over the firstborn male of the household; the child was thus redeemed from sacred duties to enter the secular life.

Out of their poverty, Joseph and Mary presented a pair of turtledoves as the price of redemption. No doubt they related to the officiating priest some of the things that had happened in connection with the birth of the child, and Simeon, an old man who was awaiting the advent of the Messiah, overheard them. He then took the six-week-old baby in his arms. The picture presents the contrast of age and of youth, of one nearing the end of the journey of life and one at the beginning. The whole of the strange thing called life lies between the extremes in that picture. When that child came into the world, he brought nothing but a soul. When that old man went out of the world he took nothing but a soul. How did he meet the test of life?

Reading this narrative, we sense that it was perfectly proper for this old man to take the baby Jesus in his arms because of what he was and who he was. Simeon was described as "devout and just" and was a part of the remnant of God's people. For these people, whether in Jerusalem or in other cities of the Holy Land, the sacrificial system of the Old Testament and the spiritual teachings of the prophets were adequate preparation for the coming of Christ. In these Old Testament types and experiences, they saw Christ. The redemptive offerings, the Day of Atonement, the Passover, all spoke to them of the coming Christ. The doctors of the Law may have been dead spiritually, but these remnant people, who saw the reality contained in the Law and the Prophets, were alive to what God was doing. Their hearts were right with God. They were devout in their worship and righteous in their dealings with their fellow men.

When Scripture uses blameless or just to describe a man like Zacharias or Simeon, the word means more than just conformity to the Law, to all the commandments and ordinances; it implies the spiritual perception of the purpose of God in the Law and the Prophets.

Simeon believed in the imminence of the Messianic age. "He waited for the consolation of Israel," the Messiah, the Lord's Christ. Simeon had long searched the Scriptures and prayed and waited for the coming of the Messiah in fulfillment of prophecy. As a crowning reward of his life, God showed him that he should not die until the Christ came.

To look for the Messianic Age is a consolation to all believers in every critical time. That hope motivated the righteous in Simeon's day to hold on to the things of God despite the terrible events happening round about them. The violations of the Law of God, the iniquity, immorality, and injustice of their day, only deepened their desire for the fulfillment of prophecies concerning the advent of the Messiah. The flame of hope must have been fanned by the report spread abroad by the shepherds of the events at Bethlehem just forty days before.

A similar hope is beating in many hearts today, even while the darkness deepens in political, educational, moral, and spiritual things. A remnant of God's people are looking for another prophetic fulfillment—the advent of the Messiah in glory, attended by his angels, to establish justice and peace on earth. As in Simeon's day, the message needed is, "Comfort ye, comfort ye my people."

"The Holy Ghost was upon Simeon." This describes a special experience of anointing known to a noble company of God's people in all ages. The Spirit rested upon Moses, and his face shone like that of an angel. The Spirit rested upon Samson, and he did marvelous exploits. The Spirit came upon the disciples at Pentecost, and they enjoyed power. For the Holy Spirit to rest upon a man is the highest experience God has for him.

The Spirit gave Simeon divine revelation—"it was revealed unto him by the Holy Ghost, that he should not see death, before he had seen the Lord's Christ." The word translated "revealed" is actually "a divine response." In the active tense the word means "to transact business," "to make an answer to those who seek advice." The use of the word in the passive bespeaks revelation made by God in response to the seeking of man. It shows that Simeon had received a gracious dealing from God in response to his own searching for divine guidance. Under the impulse of the Spirit, he had come to the temple and was performing his devotions when Jesus arrived. When he heard the account given by Mary and Joseph to the priest, he interrupted the process of dedication by taking the child in his arms and making a great spiritual prophecy under the inspiration of the Holy Spirit.

Simeon declared, "Mine eyes have seen thy salvation." The child is here equated with God's salvation. The neuter gender is used for the word salvation. Thus, Simeon was speaking not of the Savior but of the apparatus fitted to bring salvation. This apparatus was prepared by God for the salvation of all people. A little child who was conceived by the Holy Ghost and born of a virgin was to be the means of the deliverance of God's people. That child, by the combining in him of a divine nature and a human nature through a virgin birth, was the prepared apparatus to work out salvation for the world.

Simeon described the child as "a light to lighten the Gentiles." The "Gentiles" refers to the nations other than Israel. The child was to be the shining light that would dawn in human hearts over the whole of the earth. That light was symbolized by the Star of Bethlehem, which shone in the dark night when the Prince of Life came into a world torn by avarice, hatred, and war. The darkness of nineteen centuries has not been able to overcome that light, nor can the darkness of evil forces today extinguish the light of hope, faith, and love kindled by the coming of Jesus Christ.

Simeon declared the child to be "the glory of thy people Israel." That an Israelite should first mention

Christ as the means of enlightening the heathen and then emphasize the glory of Israel was an unusual order in pre-Christian times and thinking. Simeon must have understood that Israel's conversion would be realized only after the enlightenment of the heathen and the calling out of the church. He saw that the fall of Israel would be the riches of the Gentiles and that Israel's restoration will be comparable to a resurrection from the dead for the whole of humanity.

As Joseph and Mary marveled at the things spoken of their child by Simeon, they were blessed by him, and heard God's purpose for the child. Simeon addressed Mary with the words, "This child is set for the fall and rising again of many in Israel." This was an application of the prophecy of Isaiah that the Christ was to be a rock of offense, causing the fall of many in Israel (Isa 8:14).

Two kinds of persons were involved; first there were those who would apprehend Christ as the Rock and find in him a spiritual sanctuary; second, those who would reject him and find him a stumbling stone and a rock of offense (cf. Acts 4:11; 1 Pet 2:7, 8). The very order of Simeon's prophecy foretold that Israel would believe in this child.

Then Simeon announced that the child was "for a sign which shall be spoken against ... that the thoughts of many hearts may be revealed." This also was a quotation from Isaiah (7:14). Never has there been a sign more "spoken against" than that of the virgin birth and its attestation to the deity of Jesus Christ, namely, that he is God with us, or Emmanuel. It was attacked by Porphyry and Celsus and other ancients, and many unbelievers center their attacks upon it today. It is a sign that reveals the attitude of human hearts. Let a man be confronted with Christ as a supernatural person, one born without a human father, brought into the world through the womb of a virgin, as the apparatus of redemption, and he will reveal his own heart's condition by his attitude toward this supernatural Christ. He will either accept him or reject him. Christ is the touchstone of human hearts.

Simeon suggested to Mary, "A sword shall pierce through thy own soul also." He did not leave the parents upon the mount of elevation but included a drop of bitterness through the prophecy that this helpless baby was to be the suffering and dying Messiah. As a sword would pierce his heart, so figuratively a sword of suffering would pierce Mary's heart. Here Simeon looked across three decades to a picture of a man hanging on a cross, dying for the sins of his people, and suffering the penalty of the Law, thus emptying death of its sting and the Law of its curse. He also saw Mary standing by that cross, pierced in heart at the suffering of her child.

When Simeon saw the Lord's Christ, he took him up in his arms and blessed God, saying, "Lord, now lettest thou thy servant depart in peace, according to thy word." This taking Jesus into his arms was an act of the will by Simeon. The Spirit had prepared him to meet Jesus at the correct moment and had providentially brought them together. There are critical moments in life when everything depends upon immediate submission to the impulse of the Spirit. Thus Jesus was driven by the Spirit into the wilderness, to be tempted of the devil. Thus Simeon was driven under the impulse of the Spirit into the temple, and when he was confronted with the Christ child, it was necessary to receive him into his arms, not doubting because of the poverty, the humility, or the insignificance of this family. This was Simeon's one opportunity to see the Lord's Christ. When the divine illumination concerning Christ comes to us, we too must act immediately in submission and receive the Christ.

Simeon accepted the baby Jesus as the Christ of God. There is a remarkable identity in the Greek between this phrase and Peter's confession, "Thou art the Christ of God." Simeon identified this baby with the pre-existent Lord of Glory, with the Christ of prophecy, the Incarnate God, the Savior who was to work out the deliverance of the nations. What an act of faith that was! We know far more of Jesus through the New Testament revelation than Simeon ever could have known from the Old Testament prophecy, but do we embrace him in the arms of faith as the Lord's Christ as Simeon did? If we do, we will rejoice as did Simeon on that occasion.

The *nunc dimittis* of Simeon emphasizes the end of a long vigil of waiting. "Lord, now lettest thou thy servant depart in peace." Blessedness and peace were his portion. Simeon represented himself as a sentinel whom his master had placed in an elevated position and charged to look for the appearance of the star. Now he sees his long-desired star. He proclaims its rising, and he asks to be relieved from the post he has occupied so long. At the opening of Aeschylus's *Agamemnon*, a sentinel, set to watch for the appearing of fire that was to announce the taking of Troy, beholds at last the signal so impatiently expected, and he sings at once, both of the victory of Greece and of his own release. Thus Simeon describes himself as free, released from the heavy burden of life.

✦

The Men Who Missed Christmas

James Montgomery Boice

Few experiences in life are more tragic than missing something important when there was no real need to miss it. Yet that is the experience of many, many people. It is the experience of those who missed the first Christmas, and also of those who miss Christmas today.

The first of the men who missed Christmas was the innkeeper. The Bible does not mention this man explicitly. Probably by the time the story of the birth of Jesus Christ was put into writing no one remembered who he was; there was no reason to remember him. Still there certainly was an innkeeper, for when the Bible tells us that Mary "brought forth her firstborn son, and wrapped him in swaddling clothes, and laid him in a manger; because there was no room for them in the inn" (Luke 2:7 KJV), the verse implies the existence of this man. The point of the reference is that in the hustle and bustle of the season the innkeeper missed the most important birth in history.

He should not have missed it, of course. He should not have missed it simply because he was so close to it. The decree of the Emperor Augustus brought the family of Jesus to his town, Bethlehem. Mary and Joseph stood on his doorstep, perhaps even entered his waiting room, stood before his desk. The child was born in his stable, almost under his nose. And yet his preoccupation with his business kept him from it.

This dramatized account of the innkeeper's reasoning comes from a book by the distinguished American writer Frederick Buechner:

> "I speak to you as men of the world," said the Innkeeper. "Not as idealists but as realists. Do you know what it is like to run an inn—to run a business, a family, to run anything in this world for that matter, even your own life? It is like being lost

in a forest of a million trees," said the Innkeeper, "and each tree is a thing to be done. Is there fresh linen on all the beds? Did the children put on their coats before they went out? Has the letter been written, the book read? Is there money enough left in the bank? Today we have food in our bellies and clothes on our backs, but what can we do to make sure that we will have them still tomorrow? A million trees. A million things. ... Finally we have eyes for nothing else, and whatever we see turns into a thing." (The Magnificent Defeat, pp. 66, 67)

The world is filled with such persons today—materialistic men, women, and children who miss the meaning of Christmas simply because their business, parties, Christmas cards, trees, and tinsel seem too pressing. Were this not so, there would not be so many grim faces in our stores or so many tired people in our churches in December.

Do not think that the Christmas story is merely speaking to non-Christians at this point. It is probably not speaking to them much at all. Who would berate Caesar Augustus for missing Christmas? He was too far away. There was no possibility of his finding it. No one would berate the Greeks or countless others. The story speaks rather to Christians, for they are the ones who should take note of the birth of Christ deeply and yet often do not.

A number of years ago a minister named A. W. Tozer was concerned about the feverish materialism of Christians in our age. He wrote this about it:

> Every age has its own characteristics. Right now we are in an age of religious complexity. The simplicity which is in Christ is rarely found among us. In its stead are programs, methods, organizations and a world of nervous activities which occupy time and attention but can never satisfy the longing of the heart. The shallowness of our inner experience, the hollowness of our worship, and that servile imitation of the world which marks our promotional methods all testify that we, in this day, know God only imperfectly, and the peace of God scarcely at all. (The Pursuit of God, p. 17)

He added,

> If we would find God amid all the religious externals we must first determine to find him, and then

proceed in the way of simplicity. Now as always
God discovers himself to "babes" and hides himself in thick darkness from the wise and the pru-
dent. We must simplify our approach to him.

The second man who missed Christmas was Herod,
king of Judea, or, to put it more accurately, an under-
king of a border province of the far-flung Roman Empire.
There was nothing likable about Herod. He was a sly old
fox, guilty of murdering many, including at least one wife
and three sons. He probably had no religion and was a
cynic. He knew the traditions of Israel, but he only half
believed them if he believed them at all. Yet he should
have found Christmas, if only because he had such a large
stake in the outcome.

Matthew is the one who tells us Herod's story. Herod
was at home in Jerusalem when news reached him that
wise men had come from the east. They were asking
where they could find the king of the Jews, the one born
recently. Herod was well aware that they were talking
about the Messiah, and he knew of no Messiah. Talk like
that was dangerous. Herod therefore called the religious
leaders to find out where the future king should be born.
After he had found out he called the wise men themselves

and persuaded them to report to him if their search in Bethlehem proved fruitful.

"Go and search diligently for the young child; and when ye have found him, bring me word again, that I may come and worship him also" (Matt 2:8 KJV). It was a sly maneuver; murder, not worship, was in the old king's heart. It was a great pity also, for Herod knew of the birth, knew its significance. He missed it through the encrusted habit of greed and self-interest.

Today many people miss practically everything good in life because of greed and self-interest. They miss friendship, beauty, love, good times, and happiness. And many miss Jesus. Jesus said, "What shall it profit a man, if he shall gain the whole world, and lose his own soul?" (Mark 8:36 KJV). Real self-interest lies in finding the one who loves us and died to be our Savior.

There was another group of persons who missed Christmas. These were the religious leaders, the chief priests and the scribes. They of all men should not have missed the birth of Christ, for they had the Scriptures. They were the ones who could tell Herod where the Christ was to be born. They knew it was in Bethlehem. Yet they did not leave their own homes or the palace to investigate his arrival.

What kept these men from going along with the wise men? We do not know for certain, of course. But it might have been their pride in the fact that Herod had called them instead of others and that they had been able to give the right answer to his question.

We see this in the religious world. There are sectors of the church in which almost any Bible question will receive a right answer. Yet in many of these places there is no real hunger after God; the vital, joyous, and rewarding reality of the presence of the Lord Jesus Christ is lacking. Knowing the content of the Bible is not enough. To be all that God intends him to be, a person must see beyond the Book to its Author.

Yet though many did not find Christmas, some did. They were not the thousands who were engrossed in the countless details of materialistic lives. They were just poor people who were looking to God and to whom God came.

The shepherds, for instance, were not important in the social structure of the ancient East. Most people thought poorly of them. They were not even able to testify in a court of law, for their testimony was considered unreliable. And yet they saw the angels. The wise men also found Christmas. They were not even Jews—and everybody knew that God's promised salvation was of the Jews. Yet the wise men saw the star. Finally there were those like Simeon and Anna, poor but saintly people who like many others "looked for redemption in Jerusalem" (Luke 2:38 KJV). No one would have given a second thought to these poor people. They were not important. Yet they saw and even held God's treasure.

Why did these people find Christmas? The first answer is that they were honest enough to admit their need of a Savior. The self-sufficient would never have made the trip to the manger; they do not do it today. These people knew they needed a Savior. Second, they were also humble enough to receive the Lord Jesus Christ when he came. No doubt there were levels of comprehension. Perhaps the shepherds, or the wise men, or even Simeon and Anna did not understand very much. But whatever they understood they received, for we are told in each case that they praised God for the birth of the Lord.

The wise men, whether they be shepherds or magi, are the ones who acknowledge their need and humble themselves enough to receive the Lord Jesus Christ as their Savior. These, and only these, find Christmas.

✧

Ongoing Incarnation

Philip Yancey

More than two centuries before the Reformation, a theological debate broke out that pitted theologian Thomas Aquinas against an upstart from Britain, John Duns Scotus. In essence, the debate circled around the question, "Would Christmas have occurred if humanity had not sinned?"

Whereas Aquinas viewed the Incarnation as God's remedy for a fallen planet, his contemporary saw much more at stake. For Duns Scotus, the Word becoming flesh as described in the prologue to John's Gospel must surely represent the Creator's primary design, not some kind of afterthought or Plan B. Aquinas pointed to passages emphasizing the Cross as God's redemptive response to a broken relationship. Duns Scotus cited passages from Ephesians and Colossians on the cosmic Christ, in whom all things have their origin, hold together, and move toward consummation.

Did Jesus visit this planet as an accommodation to human failure or as the center point of all creation? Duns Scotus and his school suggested that Incarnation was the underlying motive for Creation, not merely a correction to it. Perhaps God spun off this vast universe for the singular purpose of sharing life and love, intending all along to join its very substance. "Eternity is in love with the inventions of time," wrote the poet William Blake.

Ultimately the church decided that both approaches had biblical support and could be accepted as orthodox. Though most theologians tended to follow Aquinas, in recent years prominent Catholics such as Karl Rahner have taken a closer look at Duns Scotus. Perhaps evangelicals should, too.

The evangelical tradition emphasizes the Atonement and Christ's life within us. We urge children to "accept Jesus into your heart," an image both comforting and confusing to a child. More pietistic strains speak of "the exchanged life" in which Christ lives both in and through the believer. Yet far more often—164 times in Paul's letters, according to one author—the New Testament uses the image of us being "in Christ." At a time when theories of the Atonement seem incomprehensible to moderns and when the Christian subculture easily shrinks into a defensive posture, we could learn from the Christ-centered view of Creation once expounded by an obscure theologian from the High Middle Ages.

When Mary gave birth to a baby in Bethlehem, she participated in an act of divine creation that continues to this day. Paul's phrase "in Christ" hints at a reality made vivid in his metaphor of the body of Christ: the church extends the Incarnation through time.

In a lovely sermon to his students at Oxford, Austin Farrer asked the natural question that arises when applying Paul's lofty metaphor to the life of the church: "But what are we to do about the yawning gulf which opens between this Christhood of ours and our actual performance; our laziness, selfishness, uncleanness, triviality, and the painful absurdity of our prayers? This gulf which yawns between what Christ has made us and what we make of ourselves?"

We do, said Farrer, the very thing Jesus' disciples did: On the first day of the week, we gather to "reassemble the whole body of Christ here, not a member lacking, when the sun has risen; and have the Resurrection over again." We remind ourselves, to borrow Paul's words, that there is now no condemnation for those who are in Christ Jesus, that we are dead to sin but alive to God in Christ Jesus, that if anyone is in Christ, he is a new creation; the old has gone, the new has come (Rom. 8:1; 6:11; 2 Cor. 5:17)! In short, we confront the stunning truth that God gazes on us through the redemptive lens of his Son.

Then, assured of that new identity, we go forth to recover God's world. Duns Scotus called his approach "the Doctrine of the Absolute Primacy of Christ in the Universe." Those who root their identity in Christ have a holy mission to reclaim territory that has been spoiled. The Christian ministers to the poor and suffering not out of humanistic motives, but because they too reflect the image of God; insists on justice because God insists on it; and honors nature because it stands as God's work of art, the background setting for Incarnation.

Not long ago I had a conversation with Makoto Fujimura, an esteemed artist who founded the International Arts Movement to encourage Christian artists to look to their faith for inspiration. "So many contemporary artists turn to other religions, like Buddhism," he says. "I remind them that God is about creation from the book of Genesis to the book of Revelation, in which God promises to make all things new."

Among Jesus' final words, in Revelation, are these: "I am the Alpha and the Omega, the first and the last, the beginning and the end." John Duns Scotus must be smiling.

✧

Christmas Implications

L. Nelson Bell

Only by recognizing the great doctrines of the Christian faith inherent in the Christmas story can we really celebrate and appreciate the significance of the event. Take these doctrines to heart and Christmas assumes its real meaning. Ignore them and you have merely another holiday.

Standing at the forefront is the Incarnation, the fact that God came into the world in human form, as Emmanuel, "God with us." Jesus Christ the incarnate God in the subsequent years of his life on earth demonstrated this marvelous truth for all to see.

To the questioning Philip he said, "Have I been with you so long, and yet you do not know me, Philip? He who has seen me has seen the Father. ... Do you not believe that I am in the Father and the Father in me? The words that I say to you I do not speak on my own authority; but the Father who dwells in me does his works" (John 14:9, 10).[8]

The Christmas story not only proclaims the Incarnation; it also tells how God descended from heaven to earth and came into time as we know it. Mary "was found to be with child of the Holy Spirit" (Matt. 1:18b). Luke records that when the angel visited her to tell her that she would bear a son, she asked, "How can this be, since I have no husband?" The angel answered, "The Holy Spirit will come upon you, and the power of the Most High will overshadow you; therefore the child to be born will be called holy, the Son of God" (Luke 1:34, 35).

The Virgin Birth is a part of the Christmas story, a wonderful part, a beautiful part. How like our God to perform his wonders in a supernatural way! One of the first lessons a Christian should learn is that "with God

---

8. Scripture quotations in this article are from the Revised Standard Version.

nothing will be impossible" (Luke 1:37), an affirmation made by the angel with reference to the Virgin Birth.

Not only does the Christmas story tell us of the Incarnation and the Virgin Birth; it also declares the purpose of Christ's coming. To Joseph the angel said: "You shall call his name Jesus [Savior], for he will save his people from their sins" (Matt 1:21); and to the fearful shepherds he said, "Be not afraid; for behold, I bring you good news of a great joy which will come to all the people; for to you is born this day in the city of David a Savior, who is Christ the Lord" (Luke 2:10, 11).

The Atonement is God's means for dealing with the guilt and penalty of sin and makes possible the "good news," the Gospel. Jesus Christ, the Son of God, came into the world for the specific purpose of saving sinners. This good news is relevant for men of all generations. It is utterly relevant for today!

Look around us. Consider America: Four or five million alcoholics and about twenty million family members affected by their plight; more children the victims of broken homes than ever before; more crime and lawlessness than ever in the history of our country; greed, lust, and violence on every hand. Is this a Great Society? It might well be called a sick society. But Christmas is the

story of One who came into the world to save sinners—
to redeem us back to God. No wonder that the Gospel is
called the "Good News"! The wonder is that so few know
it, so few speak of it, so few believe it.

The inability of many people to recognize their plight
and to acknowledge God's loving provision for that plight
is evidence of the power of Satan, who blinds the minds
and hearts of men so that they neither see nor believe.
For such persons Christmas is merely a day for celebration and revelry.

For the Christian, however, the celebration of our
Lord's birth is a time to consider anew the fact of Calvary
and the atonement for sin Christ wrought out on the
cross. The Bethlehem story, the cross, and the empty
tomb are bound together by the strongest ties. The sin-
fulness of man is exceeded by the love of God expressed
in the redeeming work of his Son.

Christmas reminds us of the miraculous. God, the God
of creation, is above and beyond that which he created. In
his intervention in human history, it was inevitable that
his supernaturalness should be manifested. It could not
have been otherwise. Not only was this birth the birth of
his Son in human form; it was also in many other ways a
divine intervention in time and space.

Astronomers generally agree that the star that led the wise men from the East and finally stopped over the Bethlehem manger cannot be explained as a natural phenomenon. But for the Magi it was so real that it led them to the manger.

In our sophistication today we discount what cannot be demonstrated by science. The star that appeared in the East was real to those who sensed its significance and followed it; and when they saw it hovering over Bethlehem, it was a source of great joy.

Woven through the Christmas story there are angelic beings. An angel appeared to the shepherds announcing the birth of the Savior. An angelic host suddenly appeared "praising God and saying, 'Glory to God in the highest, and on earth peace among men with whom he is pleased!' " (Luke 2:13b, 14). An angel appeared to Joseph in a dream and said, "Rise, take the child and his mother, and flee to Egypt, and remain there till I tell you; for Herod is about to search for the child, to destroy him" (Matt 2:13); and, later, an angel appeared to tell Joseph that Herod was dead and could no longer harm the child.

Gabriel, the angel who appeared to Daniel to instruct him, came now to Zechariah to tell him of the coming birth of his son, John. It was also Gabriel who appeared to Mary with the stupendous news that she was to be the mother of the Son of God.

Of Gabriel, so prominent in the Christmas story, we know only that he is an angel who stands in the presence of God—a supernatural being with a heavenly message of the greatest earthly importance. How little we grasp the reality of angels! In the Christmas story there is an ever-recurring reminder of those unseen beings, some of whom encamp "around those who fear him, and [deliver] them" (Ps 34:7).

Again and again the Scriptures remind us that the advent of Jesus Christ was a fulfillment of general and specific prophecies. Without the Old Testament we could never understand the New. Without fulfilled prophecy, our expectation of the yet unfulfilled would be dimmer or absent.

Finally, the Christmas story is a constant reminder of the wisdom of God's timing. Jesus came into the world "in the fulness of time," when three factors combined to help carry out God's purpose: relative peace imposed by the law and order of Rome and made effective by her communicating roads; the culture of Greece and the beauty and universality of its language, in which the New Testament was to be written; and the Hebrew nation, to which had been given the revelation of God's divine laws and prophetic plans.

To celebrate Christmas we must realize who was born, what he came to do, and how the hope of the world rests in receiving him as Savior and Lord, King of kings, and Lord of lords.

✦

Why I Celebrate Christmas

Helmut Thielicke

T hough Christmas is the festival of light and is celebrated with many lights, it often seems to me that it
is not much more than a shadow—the shadow of a Figure
who has long since passed by.

It is true, of course, that even the cast shadow has in
it a certain greatness. At any rate, it indicates the con-
tours of a reality that even the unsentimental "man of
today," who prides himself upon his objectivity, somewhat shamefacedly calls love. At Christmas we are kind
to one another, we emphasize the element of community,

and enjoy ourselves. The antagonisms that keep thrusting themselves upon us are walled off for a few moments with air cushions, and for a short time the gentle law of kindness reigns.

The true greatness becomes evident when we consider what a miracle it is after all that these images of the shepherds, mother Mary seeking shelter, and the humble stable should be capable of transforming our whole point of view for even a few moments, that they should draw us out of the vicious circle of our daily routine and make us think of our suffering, forsaken, needy fellow men.

For a few moments we are troubled by the thought that anybody should be obliged to spend Christmas Eve without its lights on the lonely sea, that anybody should be walking the streets alone with nothing and nobody to call his own, not even a future. It is the greatness of this shadow that can arouse such sadness and concern.

But an irony, or better, a sadness that escapes into irony, appears when we measure the shadow by the original Figure who cast it.

For what is a love that no longer emanates from immediate contact with him who "is" love, but lives in us only as a kind of memory, a mere distant echo? Our everyday speech is sometimes capable of reducing this bizarre shadow of a vanished love and a fleeting joy to a grotesque caricature. I often think how absurd it is for us to say, "Have sunshine in your heart!" or "Wake up happy in the morning!" It is pathetic to see the yearnings that these expressions betray, but at the same time it is quite foolish to put them in the form of imperatives. How can I possibly go about getting the sun into my heart?

Obviously, the sun can be there in my heart only if it shines upon me and then the brightness in my heart is a reflection of it. But how in the world can I "produce" the sun?

A person who invents imperatives like these strikes me as being someone who has lost the real thing and finds himself walking around in the darkness where he is compelled to vegetate without love and without joy. So he says to himself: "I cannot live without these basic elements of human life; therefore I must produce them synthetically, namely, by an act of my will." So he summons his heart to produce the sun. The futility of such an attempt is like the fool's trying to catch sunlight in a sack.

When I am asked why as a Christian I celebrate Christmas, my first reply is that I do so because something has happened to me, and therefore—but only as I am receptive and give myself to it—something now can happen in me.

There is a Sun "that smiles at me," and I can run out of the dark house of my life into the sunshine (as Luther once put it). I live by virtue of the miracle that God is not merely the mute and voiceless ground of the universe, but that he comes to me down in the depths. I see this in him who lay in the manger, a human child, and yet different from us all.

And even though at first I look upon it only as a lovely colored picture, seeing it with the wondering eyes of a child, who has no conception whatsoever of the problem of the personhood of God and the Trinity and the metaphysical problems of time and eternity, I see that he, whom "all the universe could not contain," comes down into the world of little things, the little things of my life, into the world of homelessness and refugees, a world where there are lepers, lost sons, poor old ladies, and men and women who are afraid, a world in which men cheat and are cheated, in which men die and are killed.

Crib and cross: these are the nethermost extremes of life's curve; no man can go any deeper than this; and he traversed it all. I do not need first to become godly and noble before I can have part in him. For there are no depths in my life where he has not already come to meet me, no depths to which he has not been able to give meaning by surrounding them with love and making them the place where he visits me and brings me back home.

Once it happened, once in the world's history it happened, that someone came forward with the claim that he was the Son of God and the assertion "I and the Father are one," and that he proved the legitimacy of that claim, not by acting like a supernatural being or stunning men with his wisdom or communicating knowledge of higher worlds, but rather by proving his claim through the depths to which he descended. A Son of God who defends his title with the arguments that he is the brother of even the poorest and the guilty and takes their burden upon himself: this is a fact one can only note, and shake one's head in unbelief—or one must worship and adore. There is no other alternative. I must worship. That's why I celebrate Christmas.

What, then, is the good of all the usual religious froth? What do these pious sentimentalities actually accomplish? Aren't they really "opium"? What difference does it make if I see in God the Creator of the galaxies and solar systems and the microcosm of the atom? What is this God of macrocosm and microcosm to me if my conscience torments me, if I am repining in loneliness, if anxiety is strangling me? What good is that kind of a God to me, a poor wretch, a heap of misery, for whom nobody cares, whom people in the subway stare at without ever seeing?

The "loving Father above the starry skies" is up there in some monumental headquarters while I sit in a fox-hole somewhere on this isolated front (cut off from all communication with the rear), somewhere on this trash heap, living in lodgings or a mansion, working at a stupid job that gives me misery or at an executive's desk that is armored with two anterooms—what do I get out of it when someone says, "There is a Supreme Intelligence that conceived the creation of the world, devised the law of cause and effect, and maneuvered the planets into their orbits?" All I can say to that is, "Well, you don't say! A rather bold idea, but almost too good to be true," and go on reading my newspaper or turn on the television. For that certainly is not a message by which I could live.

But if someone says, "There is Someone who knows you, Someone who grieves when you go your own way, and it cost him something (namely, the whole expenditure of life between the crib and the cross!) to be the star to which you can look, the staff by which you can walk, the spring from which you can drink"—when someone says that to me, then I prick up my ears and listen. For if it is true, really true, that there is Someone who is interested in me and shares my lot, then this can suddenly change everything that I hoped for and feared before. This could mean a revolution in my life, at any rate a revolution in my judgment and knowledge of things.

In other words, I should say that all the atheists, nihilists, and agnostics are right at one point, and that is when they say that the course of history gives us no basis whatever for any knowledge of God and the so-called higher thoughts that govern our world. But Christmas teaches us that, if we wish to know God, we must in our relationship to the world begin at a completely different end, namely, that we do not argue from the structure of the world to God, but rather from the Child in the manger to the mystery of the world, to the mystery of the world in which the manger exists.

Then I see in this Child that in the background of this world there is a Father. I see that love reigns above and in the world, even when I cannot understand this governance, and I am tormented by the question of how God can permit such tragic things to happen.

But if the manifestation of love conquers me at one point, namely, where Jesus Christ walked this Earth and loved it, then I can trust that it will also be the message at those points in the story of life that I cannot understand. Even a child knows that his father is not playing tricks on him in a way that is seemingly incompatible with love. The highest love is almost always incognito, and therefore we must trust it.

Let me put it in the form of an illustration. If I look at a fine piece of fabric through a magnifying glass, I find that it is perfectly clear around the center of the glass, but around the edges it tends to become distorted. But this does not mislead me into thinking that the fabric itself is confused at this point. I know that this is caused by an optical illusion and therefore by the way in which I am looking at it. And so it is with the miracle of knowledge that is bestowed upon me by the Christmas event: If I see the world through the medium of the Good News, then the center is clear and bright.

There I see the miracle of the love that descends to the depths of life. On the periphery, however, beyond the

Christmas light, confusion and distortion prevail. The ordered lines grow tangled, and the labyrinthine mysteries of life threaten to overwhelm us. Therefore our sight, which grows aberrant as it strays afield, must recover its perspective by returning to the thematic center. The extraordinary thing is that the mystery of life is not illuminated by a formula, but rather by another mystery, namely, the News, which can only be believed and yet is hardly believable, that God has become man and that now I am no longer alone in the darkness.

That's why I celebrate Christmas.

✧

The Blessed Evangelical Mary

Timothy George

In his *History of the Reformation in Scotland,* John Knox described an incident from his early life as a Protestant. Having been delivered from "the puddle of papistry," as he called it, he was taken as a prisoner and forced to row in a French galley ship for 19 months.

> Soon after the arrival [of the galley ship] at Nantes, ... a glorious painted Lady was brought in to be kissed and, amongst others, was presented to one of the Scottishmen then chained. He gently said, "Trouble me not; such an idol is a curse; and

therefore I will not touch it." The Patron and the Arguesyn, with two officers, having the chief charge of all such matters, said, "Thou shalt handle it"; and so they violently thrust it in his face and put in betwixt his hands; who seeing the extremity, took the idol, and advisedly looking about, he cast it in the river, and said, "Let our Lady now save herself: she is light enough; let her learn to swim!"

Some scholars believe the "Scottishman" involved in this incident was none other than Knox himself. Most evangelical Protestants can relate to this story, for we belong to a tradition of piety decisively shaped by the likes of Knox. We have an almost instinctive distrust of Mary. Why?

First, we find no biblical warrant for the kind of devotion to Mary that flourishes among many of the Catholic faithful. Mary's perpetual virginity (the belief that she had no children after Jesus and remained a virgin throughout her life), immaculate conception (that she was born without the stain of original sin), and bodily assumption (that she was taken body and soul into heaven after she died without seeing corruption) are extrabiblical beliefs that cannot be traced to the earliest historical memory of the church.

To be sure, if God had wanted to raise Mary and take her directly to heaven without her waiting for the general resurrection, he certainly could have done so. We know that God took Elijah into heaven without death. But to declare this teaching an infallible dogma, as Pope Pius XII did in 1950, creates an even deeper divide between Catholics and other Christians. This is why Brother Roger Shutz, the Swiss Protestant founder of the Taizé community, felt it necessary to travel to Rome to urge the pope not to take this step. Brother Roger rightly saw that this act would drive Christians further away from one another.

Protestants believe that an undue extolling of Mary obscures, if it does not contradict, the sole sufficiency of Jesus Christ as the unique Savior and only mediator between God and human beings. Recent efforts to have Mary officially recognized as *mediatrix* of all graces, or as *coredemptrix* with Christ himself—though unsuccessful thus far—have only added to the fear that lifting up Mary can only result in bringing down Jesus.

So the question remains: does Protestantism have a place for the Blessed Virgin Mary or, like Knox of the galleys, must we throw her overboard once and for all? Without compromising the Reformation principles of *sola gratia, sola fide,* and *sola scriptura,* can we understand and honor Mary in ways that are scripturally based and evangelically motivated? Are we to be included among those of every generation who call Jesus' mother "blessed"?

C ontemporary Protestants are wise to listen to both the Reformers' critique of Marian piety and their praise of Mary, the handmaiden of the Lord. Luther and all the Reformers strongly protested against the "abominable idolatry" of medieval Mariology. This is not too strong a term for some of the beliefs that prevailed at that time. For example, Mary was often portrayed as placating her stern son with milk from her breasts. This was one reason why Mary's milk, supposedly preserved in reliquaries throughout Europe, was so highly valued.

Mary was seen as the one who intervened with Christ on behalf of sinners—she was a mediator with the Mediator. In this vein, various texts of Scripture were rewritten with a Marian slant: 1 Corinthians 15:22 became, "as in Eve all die, so also in Mary shall all be made alive." And John 3:16 was rendered: "Mary so loved the world ... that she gave her only-begotten son for the salvation of the world." And, anticipating feminist liturgies half a millennium later, the Lord's Prayer began: "Our Mother who art in heaven, give us our daily bread."

This kind of exaggerated devotion, the Reformers held, does not praise the virgin mother of God but in fact slanders her by making her into an idol. Nowhere is the Protestant reaction to Marian excess more cogently put than in Philipp Melanchthon's "Apology of the Augsburg Confession" (1530):

> Some of us have seen a certain monastic theologian ... urge this prayer upon a dying man, "Mother of grace, protect us from the enemy and receive us in the hour of death." Granted that blessed Mary prays for the church, does she receive souls in death, does she overcome death, does she give life? What does Christ do if Mary does all this? ... The fact of the matter is that in popular estimation the blessed virgin has replaced Christ. People have invoked her, trusted in her mercy, and sought to appease Christ as though he were not a propitiator but only a terrible judge and avenger.

Yet alongside this critique the Reformers expressed a positive devotion to Mary. Both Zwingli and Bullinger defended the Ave Maria not as a prayer to Mary but as an expression of praise in honor of her. (In fact, many medieval versions of the Ave Maria did not include the phrase most repugnant to Reformers: "pray for us sinners, now and in the hour of our death.")

Calvin too refers to Mary as "the treasurer of grace," the one who kept faith as a deposit. Through her, Calvin says, we have received this precious gift from God. "She deserves to be called blessed, for God has accorded her a singular distinction, to prepare his son for the world, in whom she was spiritually reborn." In 1521, Luther, sequestered in the Wartburg, prepared for press his commentary on the Magnificat. Mary, he wrote, is the embodiment of God's unmerited grace.

She is called blessed not because of her virginity or even her humility, but because she was chosen as the person and place where God's glory would enter most deeply into the human story. "I am only the workshop in which God operates," Luther has Mary say. As T. S. Eliot would say in Four Quartets, Mary is "the place of impossible union where past and future are conquered and reconciled in incarnation."

Above all, the Reformers recognize Mary as the one who hears the Word of God and responds in faith, and thus is justified by faith alone. Mary was a disciple of Christ before she was his mother, for had she not believed, she would not have conceived. Mary's faith too is not the achievement of merit, but the gift of divine grace. This means that when we praise and love Mary, it is God whom we praise for his gracious favor to his chosen handmaid.

Honoring Mary certainly doesn't come naturally to Protestants. For complex historical reasons, to be a Protestant has meant not to be a Roman Catholic. To worship Jesus means not to honor Mary, even if such honor is biblically grounded and theologically sound. But, as the Reformers were quick to point out, Mary is the embodiment of grace alone and faith alone, and thus contemporary Protestants, along with the Reformers, should highly extol Mary in our theology and worship.

In 1886 A. Stewart Walsh published *Mary: The Queen of the House of David and Mother of Jesus*. A magnum opus of 626 pages, it reads somewhat like an extensive Harlequin romance of Mary's life. Highly romanticized and fictionalized, it is a paean of praise to motherhood in general, of which Mary is the chief exemplar. Near the end of this fanciful work, however, there is this plea for a proper evangelical recognition of Mary:

> No friend of the divine Son can dethrone Him by honoring her aright: indeed, as He Himself did. It was of Him she spoke when exclaiming: My soul doth rejoice in God my Savior! Can one truly honor Him and despise and ignore the woman who gave Him human birth? Can one have His mind and forget her for whom love was uppermost to Him in His supreme last hours? Can one honor her aright and yet dethrone the son whom she enthroned? She bore Him, then lived for Him. She honored herself in bearing Him, and was His mother, His teacher and His disciple. He revered her, she worshiped Him.

The New Testament portrays Mary as among the last at the cross, and among the first in the Upper Room. She bridges not only the Old and New Testaments at Jesus' birth, but also the close of his earthly ministry and the birth of the church. It is significant that in Eastern iconography, Mary is never depicted alone, but always with Christ, the apostles, and the saints.

At the foot of the cross, Mary represents the church as a faithful remnant. Already before the Reformation, Mary was seen as the archetype of the remnant church: her faithfulness alone kept the church intact during Christ's suffering on the cross.

When all of the disciples (including Peter!) had fled in fear, Mary remained true to Christ and his word. Her fidelity unto the Cross showed that the true faith could be preserved in one sole individual, and thus Mary became the mother of the (true remnant) church. This is why the Reformers honored Mary.

Today, perhaps more than ever, the image of Mary under the cross speaks to the church, which is increasingly the persecuted church. Some interpreters have found an allusion to Mary in the book of Revelation's depiction of the pregnant woman pursued and persecuted by an enormous red dragon (Rev 12:1–5). Whether or not this is a correct interpretation, there is no doubt that the Mary of the Gospels stands in solidarity with all believers in Jesus who also live under the shadow of the Cross, including many whose lives are at risk today because of their witness for Christ.

My favorite religious painting shows Mary standing under the cross. It is the famous painting by Matthias

Grünewald from the Isenheim Altarpiece produced on the eve of the Reformation. A copy of this painting hung over the desk of Karl Barth.

The painting shows John the Baptist pointing with his long bony finger to Jesus writhing in the agonies of death. In faded red letters, in Latin, are the words "He must increase, I must decrease." John points not to himself nor to anyone else, but to Christ alone. This is the task of all true ministers of the Gospel, indeed of every true Christian. We say to those we meet, "Don't believe in me, believe in him. Don't follow me, follow him. He is 'the Lamb of God who takes away the sin of the world' " (John 1:29).

The Blessed Virgin Mary is also a prominent figure in this painting. She too stands under the cross—not only with John the beloved disciple (as usually depicted), but also with John the Baptist. She joins him in pointing others to Jesus, representing the church in its primary call to discipleship and witness.

This is the Mary Protestants can and should embrace. We do not think of the mother of God, an object of devotion by herself, in isolation from her son. We need not go through Mary in order to get to Jesus, but we can join with Mary in pointing others to him. This, more than anything else, will honor her as she honored him. As the Anglican poet-chaplain of World War I, G. A. Studdert-Kennedy, expressed it in his poem "Good Friday Falls on Lady Day":

> And has our Lady lost her place?
> Does her white star burn dim?
> Nay, she has lowly veiled her face
> Because of Him.
>
> Men give to her the jeweled crown,
> And robe with broidered rim,
> But she is fain to cast them down
> Because of Him.
>
> She claims no crown from Christ apart,
> Who gave God life and limb,
> She only claims a broken heart
> Because of Him.

✧

An After-Christmas Gift

Lee Knapp

One opportunity I did not want to miss at Christmas was to serve dinner at a homeless shelter downtown. After being relegated to the church's substitute list in September, I jumped at the chance when a friend called to say she'd need me one Wednesday in mid-December. Besides wanting to get better acquainted with members of a new church we'd been attending, I had been longing for a more tangible experience of faith to round out my spiritual resumé. For too long my faith had been living in my head, with no other work to do but memorize facts about God and figure out my personal life.

Indeed, my head had become a lively Parisian salon to which a variety of voices paid regular visits. Jesus had come in recently, commanding me, "Feed my sheep," while an aging Miss America reminded me to "help people," if only to impress the judges. More often, especially since the month when I'd passed my 45th birthday, the conversation was dominated by the topic of death—specifically, mine.

After miscues in both December and January, waiting in vain for fellow church members to join me (two homeless shelters with the same name?), I was more determined than ever to do my selfless good works, even if for selfish reasons. Those mishaps, which had seemed like a supernatural test, turned out to be a kind of scavenger hunt for an after-Christmas gift God had hidden for me.

On a freezing night in February, I finally found myself at Freedom House, standing behind a long table, serving up cornbread. As more than 100 people came in from the 20-degree weather, they walked along with their trays and thanked us often. One man was handsome, except for a few missing teeth, and could have been a basketball star or banker in another time. Then came a huge man with beautifully chiseled facial features, wearing not only a knit hat but also a bulky scarf knotted on the front of his forehead, making him look like a swami or one of the three wise men. Another short, timid man with thin strands of hair plastered over his scalp in a severe left-to-right orientation shuffled by, muttering the whole time he was there, "I should be in the hospital. They wouldn't let me stay."

I was feeling a certain lightness of heart. In fact, I hadn't thought about death the whole evening. Then a tall man with a voice like a sports broadcaster came up to the serving table, directly in front of me. Would he want something? Should I think of something spiritual to say? Instead he asked, "Hey, are you all Christians?" Like a modern Elijah, in his wonderfully clear voice, he began his story.

"I want to tell y'all what happened to me. It was September 10, 1999. September 10th. I was in North Carolina lying on my bed. I know I did not fall asleep. This was not a dream. An angel came to me to show me heaven. Man, you guys, it was real. I'm telling you, it was real. There was a river, a huge river, flowing right through the middle of where I was walking, and it flowed into a fountain but never flowed out. There were lots of buildings, real architecture that was mostly white and beautiful, huge, man. You know how Jesus says 'In my Father's house there are many mansions'? Well, it's true. There are houses in heaven. And the angel was showing me around. I recognized her because it was the same one—like she was my guardian angel—who came to me 15 years ago when I tried to commit suicide. Both times I told her I wanted to stay there, but she said it was not my time. I'm telling you, guys, it was real. I didn't want to come back here, but it wasn't my time. And there were people there, not really flesh and bones, but there were men and women and children. They were kind of clear, but everyone was like a bronze color, kind of see-through bronze or something. You could definitely recognize people."

His voice began to crescendo, slightly preacher-like. His tone was prophetic. "Heaven is real, man. I'm telling you. So you gotta' keep on doin' what you're doin'. It's all worth it. Keep on doin' what you're doin'."

You could have driven a truck through my slacked jaw. The picture he painted of heaven was so vivid and somehow strangely resonant, and his enthusiasm was infectious. Call me naïve or softheaded, but I didn't want to relegate this man's vision to the effects of a substance or mental illness, even if that were the case. I didn't care.

I chose to suspend my rationality and enter into the imaginative promise and hopefulness of what he shared. After all, the birth of Jesus sounds a little crazy, too.

The man next to me spoke first. "Have you written this down for your family?" Our prophet looked blankly at him, but with a twinge of interest while buttoning his old Navy peacoat.

I broke in and said to him, "You know, I really needed to hear you tell me this tonight. I've been worried too much about dying. Thank you. It really helped me." He looked at me and again said, "Just keep doin' good. Keep doing what you're doin'." Again, my church friend said to him, "You really need to write your vision down."

Then it hit me. I am a writer—sometimes.

I looked up at him and asked, "What's your name?"

"Derek," he answered, by now prepared to go out into the weather, his backpack in place and holding a piece of cardboard.

"Thanks, Derek, for telling me this. I'm pretty sure I was supposed to meet you tonight. I'll write it down for you."

Those of us from church swept up, got our coats, and headed downstairs to the back parking lot. I was still a little stunned and wasn't able to tell my friend Connie what had happened yet. We crept up the alley in my minivan, and ended up right next to the sidewalk in front of the shelter. Among many of the others we'd just served, there stood Derek, right next to us at the passenger window, holding a cardboard sign.

For some inexplicable reason, I very consciously and quickly looked away from him, focusing instead on the approaching traffic to my left. I just felt so useless all of a sudden—and ashamed of my self-importance and tightly wound brain. But maybe that was a good starting-over point, a way for faith and hope to come back to life. I also may have avoided any eye contact because the scary truth about our common humanity—especially on a 12 degree F. night—hit me hard as I saw him there. That may help too, to nudge my earlier misdirected intentions about good works into a more true line, and action. "Just keep doin' what you're doin'."

Once I pulled out into traffic, I did catch a glimpse of the sign he held: HOMELESS, PLEASE HELP.

I keep thinking about Derek's vision, letting my imagination take me there to see those buildings we're promised, trying to distinguish the faces in bronze that I may know, to hear the flow of that river. God knew I needed Derek's vision. I'm glad for whatever selfish reason or

Spirit-led impulse that prompted me last Christmas season, so I could be in the right Freedom House at the right time minding the cornbread to hear about it.

☆

Not Yet Home
for Christmas

Jen Pollock Michel

Carolina first left the Gaza Strip to study journalism in Toronto. At age 20, she arrived newly pregnant and, as a result, lost her scholarship—though not her valuable student visa. Without educational opportunity, she eventually went back home.

Carolina returned to Canada this March. This time, with a toddler in tow and another on the way, her travels included hungry hours on a hot bus and repeated attempts to cross the border into Egypt, where she and her child finally boarded a 12-hour flight to North America.

Carolina was fleeing hopelessness for the sliver of light that is this New World.

"In Gaza, there is no work. There is no dignity. Any day, you can die." She pauses. "But it is difficult here. Very difficult." Her immigration status hangs in the balance. She cannot know when—or if—her husband will join her.

Like the stories of the millions of refugees from Syria, Iraq, Libya, South Sudan, Eritrea, and Nigeria, Carolina's story is the Christmas story, although not in the ways we usually think. The immutable "I AM that I AM" entered a womb and took up a body. But these were not his only vulnerable acts. Jesus of Nazareth also claimed an earthly home, which, as Carolina and many others know, is less a promise of permanence and more a risk of grief. When mobility, death, divorce, ecological crisis, and war reign, there is nothing certain in life, not least a home.

"To have a home is to become vulnerable," writes James Wood in an essay for *The London Review of Books*. "Not just to the attacks of others, but to our own adventures in alienation." Wood recalls that the battle prowess of the Scythians was often attributed to the fact that they were nomads, without a home. Because "they carry their houses with them and shoot with bows from horseback," Wood writes, they were invincible, leaving behind no settlements for enemies to attack. Without a home, one has less to lose. With a home, happiness is the rug that can be jerked, without warning, from under our feet.

But we are hardwired for home and for the refuge it promises. The Creation narrative introduces a home-making, home-keeping God, who lays a feast and welcomes guests. Twice in Genesis 2, we hear that God "puts" Adam and Eve in the Garden of Eden. The second time, Scripture doesn't use the common term for "put" (like putting our shoes in the closet), but instead uses a word that connotes rest and safety. They are *put* in the Garden in the same way God *put* Lot outside the city before he rained sulfur and fire on Sodom (Gen. 19:16), that he *put* the Israelites in the Promised Land as a gift of rest (Deut. 3:20; 12:10; 25:19).

This Hebrew word for *put* can also refer to something dedicated to God, like the manna that was "put" in the ark of the covenant. Old Testament scholar John Sailhamer suggests that the author of Genesis intends both meanings in verse 15: "The man was 'put' into the Garden where he could 'rest' and be 'safe,' and the man was 'put' into the Garden 'in God's presence' where he could have fellowship with God."

Our first human parents were given a home and invited to sit and stay awhile. But they, and we, have chosen rebellion. So the drama of life unfolds not at home, but in exile. "Home is the mouth of a shark," writes Warsan Shire, a Somali poet. "Home is the barrel of the gun / and no one would leave home / unless home chased you to the shore." Because of sin, we are all on foot now. To be human is to be homesick, longing for paradise lost.

Christmas is a time when many families return home, buoyed by starry expectation for the transcendent meaning we are supposed to be finding around our tables. But our celebrations, good in their own right, do not ultimately sate our longing for home. Even in Middle America, the specter of exile haunts the human experience.

Christmas reminds us that the riskiest business of the Incarnation wasn't ultimately the manger but the cross. God exiled his own Son in order to restore home to the sinner, the sinner to home. And because the longing for home is the ache of every human heart, the good news is as deliciously true as Jesus told it in Luke 15: *Once upon a time, there was a patient father with two rebellious sons. One came home, and a feast was laid.*

Salvation, as homecoming. Forgiveness, as eternal feast. Welcome home.

The Magi's Worship

Kent R. Hughes

In C. S. Lewis's *The Voyage of the Dawn Treader*, Lucy finds a magical book that tells of a cup, a sword, a tree, and a green hill—the Narnian equivalent to the gospel story. We are told that as the little girl read, "she was living in the story as if it were real, and all the pictures were real too. When she had got to the third page and come to the end, she said, 'That is the loveliest story I've ever read or ever shall read in my whole life. Oh, I wish I could have gone on reading it for ten years.'"

That is the way it is with the story of the Incarnation. Though we explore the same short passages year after year, we never tire of hearing the Christmas story. It is the loveliest we shall ever read.

Part of that story, of course, is the adoration of the Magi and the presence of a mysterious star as recorded in Matthew 2:1–11.

The mystery that surrounds the Magi has fueled the imaginations of millions over nearly two thousand Christmases. Not all of these imaginings have been on the mark—the most notable being that the Magi were kings and that they were three in number. The supposition that they were kings comes from an over-reading of Old Testament parallels in Psalm 72:10–11 and Isaiah 60:6, where it speaks of gift-bearing kings bowing down before him. And the idea that there were three comes from the fact that they presented Christ with three gifts: gold, frankincense, and myrrh.

From these reasonable imaginings came other "explanations" bordering on or beyond sheer fantasy. In the Western church the Magi were given the names Balthasar, Melchior, and Caspar—and several cathedrals claim to have their remains. The great Cathedral of Cologne even supplies this interesting obituary:

"Having undergone many trials and fatigues for the Gospel the three wise men met at Sewa (Sebaste in

Armenia) in AD 54 to celebrate the feast of Christmas. Thereupon, after the celebration of Mass, they died; St. Melchior on January 1st, aged 116; St. Balthasar on January 6th, aged 112; and St. Caspar on January 11th, aged 109."

(Of course, virtually no Protestant or Catholic scholars today believe this obituary or that any of the Magi's relics survive.)

What we do know of the mysterious Magi is this: They most likely came from Persia or Parthia, and were not crude pagans but religious scholars who, as part of their pursuit, studied the heavens. (We need to remember that astrology was originally connected with man's search for God, and that astrologers simply tried to find in the heavens the answer to their moral longings. They came with real, but imperfect, messianic expectations.) Philo of Alexandria, a contemporary of Jesus, indicates that he knew of both scientific magi and magi who were charlatans and magicians.

The magi of our story were probably influenced by expatriate Jews who shared their sacred writings, thus instilling in them the expectation of a coming kingly Jewish figure. New Testament scholar Raymond Brown says, "They represent the best of pagan lore and religious

perceptivity which has come to seek Jesus through revelation in nature" and are "the wise and learned among
the Gentiles."

What galvanized these Magi into action was the appearance of what the text calls a "star in the East." Like the Magi themselves, this star has spawned some brilliant and entertaining theories.

One is that the star was a supernova or "new star"—
the explosion of a faint star giving off an extraordinary
amount of light. This is only theory as there is no ancient
record of such an occurrence before Jesus' birth.

A second theory is that the star was a comet. Comets
move in elliptical paths around the sun—a few bright
ones appearing each century. According to calculations,
Halley's comet appeared around 12–11 BC, a considerable time before Jesus' birth—and a comet is not a star.
Moreover, comets were thought to herald catastrophes,
not births.

The third and most popular theory is that the star was
an unusual conjunction, or alignment, of planets. Such
a positioning took place in 7 BC, about two years before
Christ's birth. The problem is that there is no contemporary evidence for calling a conjunction a "star."

But according to verse 9, this "star," this luminous wonder, "went on before [the Magi], until it came and stood over where the child was." It moved from north to south, from Jerusalem to Bethlehem. And to rest over the very house that the child lived in, the star would have to have come very low. Unusual cosmic behavior, to be sure.

My opinion is that the star was some phenomenon functioning within the earth's atmosphere (not unlike the Shekinah glory). Note in support of this that verse 9 seems to indicate that it reappeared to the Magi after the interview with King Herod. Of course, God could have used either natural or supernatural phenomena. The point is, the star was a historical, supernatural provision—which infallibly led the Magi to the Savior.

Now our Christmas text comes alive:

"Now after Jesus was born in Bethlehem of Judea in the days of Herod the king, behold, magi from the East arrived in Jerusalem, saying, 'Where is he who has been born King of the Jews? For we saw his star in the East, and have come to worship him' " (vv. 1–2; all quotations taken from the NASB).

Whether riding camels or not, they must have been an impressive sight—for they were wealthy, noble Persians, bearing not only their great gifts but the dust

of a thousand miles. But what really electrified everyone was that these Gentiles were looking for a newborn
Jewish king! They dramatize for our imaginations and
hearts what was always implicit in biblical history—the
Christ was for Gentiles, too.

What an example, then, the Magi set in seeking Christ.
Traveling in ancient times was miserable. The exposure
and the danger from criminals shortened many lives. But
these men came because they believed. No obstacle was
too great.

Evidently the Magi's arrival in Jerusalem was a public
event. Matthew describes what happened: "And
when Herod the king heard it, he was troubled, and all
Jerusalem with him."

King Herod was "all shook up," for the literal sense
of the word translated "troubled" is "to shake" or "to
stir." The only other place the word is used in Matthew
is 14:26, where it describes the fright of the disciples
when they see Jesus coming toward them on the sea
like a water-walking ghost. The Greek version of the Old
Testament uses this word to describe Belshazzar's fright
at seeing the handwriting on the wall (Daniel 5:9). The

King James Version says, "his joints were loosed and one knee smote the other."

Herod, then, did not have a mild case of the jitters—this was theatrical in scope. And Herod's psychological imbalance further complicated the scene. He was crazy, having previously murdered his own two sons and his wife, Miriamne (she because he couldn't bear the thought of his dying first and her living without him). No wonder all Jerusalem was "shook up." No one could guess what cruel extremes he would go to next. Terror reigned in the Holy City.

In his fright, Herod called for the help of the religious establishment:

"And gathering together all the chief priests and scribes of the people, he began to inquire of them where the Christ was to be born. And they said to him, 'In Bethlehem of Judea; for so it has been written by the prophet, "And you, Bethlehem, land of Judah; are by no means least among the leaders of Judah; for out of you shall come forth a Ruler, who will shepherd My people Israel" ' " (vv. 4–6).

The answer was easy; even the common people knew it (cf. John 7:41–42). Micah 5:2 had predicted some

700 years before that the Messiah would be born in Bethlehem. Here the officials paraphrase the ancient prophecy and add a final line from 2 Samuel 5:2, "who will shepherd my people Israel," which in its context emphasizes that this one born in Bethlehem will be of the house of David. Everyone knew the answer!

And this fact sets up a supreme irony, which Matthew wants us to see: Though these religious leaders knew exactly where the Christ was to be born, none of them went along with the Magi to see if it was so. They illustrate the amazing apathy to which religious people— those who have it all, have heard it all, and can recite it all—can fall into. The scribes knew the Scripture inside out. They even numbered the letters and lines to insure careful copying. Yet Jesus said of them:

"You search the Scriptures, because you think that in them you have eternal life; and it is these that bear witness of me; and you are unwilling to come to me, that you may have life" (John 5:39–40).

It is so easy to become this way. It is a special temptation for preachers. We can be like flight announcers at the airport who, by virtue of the fact that they are constantly announcing destinations, come to believe they have been there themselves. Knowledge and words just don't do it.

And there is a Christmas danger implicit here. It is that our annual celebration of Christmas can immunize us to its reality (especially if it is our only regular exposure to the gospel). We hear just enough of the story each year to inoculate us against the real thing, so that we never really catch true Christmas fever. The most impenetrable armor against the gospel is a familiar, lifelong knowledge of it.

What are we to do? Old William Law gives the answer: "When the first spark of a desire after God arrives in thy soul, cherish it with all thy care, give all thy heart unto it. ... Follow it as gladly as the wise men of the East followed the star from heaven that appeared to them. It will do for thee as the star did for them: it will lead thee to the birth of Jesus, not in a stable at Bethlehem of Judea, but to the birth of Jesus in thine own soul."

Let's go back to Herod. He may have been crazy, but he was sly as a fox. So he dismissed the religious leaders and arranged to see the Magi:

"Then Herod secretly called the magi, and ascertained from them the time the star appeared. And he sent them to Bethlehem, and said, 'Go and make careful search for the Child; and when you have found him, report to me, that I too may come and worship him' " (vv. 7–8).

Nothing could be lower than Herod's pious pretense masking his murderous intent. No doubt he would have killed them all—the child, the parents, and the unsuspecting Magi—if they had followed through as they planned with his orders.

Mercifully, that was not to be: "And having heard the king, they went their way; and lo, the star, which they had seen in the East, went on before them, until it came and stood over where the child was. And when they saw the star, they rejoiced exceedingly, with great joy" (vv. 9–10).

The star reappeared. It stood stationary over a humble home—and then the Magi began to rejoice. We do ourselves a disservice if we limit their rejoicing to prim, restrained smiles. They rejoiced like Middle Easterners—noisy and exuberant! With excitement they dismounted, uncovered their gifts, straightened their robes and turbans, and stepped toward the entrance. I love Luther's suggestion that the humble dwelling was probably a great trial to the Magi. Had they come thousands of miles to this—a poor peasant's home outside the big city? It is a credit to their faith that they went in:

"And they came into the house and saw the child with Mary his mother; and they fell down and worshiped him; and opening their treasures they presented to him gifts of gold and frankincense and myrrh" (v. 11).

There are three things we must not overlook in this climactic verse:

First, the Magi "fell down"; they did not sit up. They knelt to the ground before the child—perhaps they even lay prone before him, expressing the inward prostration of their hearts. The picture is remarkable, and even more remarkable when we realize that these are Gentiles bowing before a Jew—and a baby at that!

Second, the picture is intensified by the additional phrase, which says they "worshiped him." The word literally means "to kiss toward," as pagans would kiss the ground before their idols. Here it bears the idea of intense adoration. They adored the Lord Jesus! All of their being was extended toward him. Think of how the sight must have affected Joseph and Mary. No doubt they flushed warmly as they watched.

Last, they "presented to him gifts of gold and frankincense and myrrh." Much has been made of the typology of these gifts, and much of it is sentimental and inaccurate.

Matthew simply wants us to see that they gave Jesus highly expensive gifts: gold, which has always been one of the rarest and most expensive of metals; frankincense, a much-valued incense extracted from the bark of trees; and myrrh, a coveted spice and perfume. They were, indeed, gifts fit for a king. The Magi gave the best they had. True worship always involves giving what we have, the very best of ourselves and possessions, to Christ.

The story of the Magi concludes with a beautiful, forthright presentation of the primacy of worship. It will never change. Christmas is a call to worship, to prostrate ourselves before Jesus. To kiss the Son, to adore him. To give him our best.

"I urge you therefore, brethren, by the mercies of God, to present your bodies a living and holy sacrifice, acceptable to God, which is your spiritual service of worship" (Rom. 12:1).

Sources

November 27: Alice Slaikeu Lawhead, "Meditation: Advent," *Christianity Today* 36, no. 15 (December 14, 1992): 17–19.

November 28: Stanley Grenz, "Meditation: Drive-through Christmas," *Christianity Today* 43, no. 14 (December 6, 1999): 74.

November 29: Katelyn Beaty, "The Poverty of Christmas," *Christianity Today* 59, no. 10 (December 2015): 25–26.

November 30: Tim Stafford, "Bethlehem on a Budget: Planning a Church Budget and the Christmas Story Share Surprising Similarities," *Christianity Today* 33, no. 18 (December 15, 1989): 34–35.

December 1: Mary Ellen Ashcroft, "Away from the Manger," *Christianity Today* 32, no. 18 (December 9, 1988): 19–20.

December 2: Wendy Alsup, "Saved through Child-Bearing: How Paul's Often Misunderstood Words in 1 Timothy Can Deepen Our Understanding of Christmas," *Christianity Today* 60, no. 10 (December 2016): 55–57.

December 3: Leigh C. Bishop, "Christmas in Afghanistan," *Christianity Today* 53, no. 12 (December 2009): 36.

December 4: Mary Ellen Ashcroft, "Meditation: Gift Wrapping God," *Christianity Today* 41, no. 14 (December 8, 1997): 32–33.

December 5: Eugene H. Peterson, "Christmas Shame," *Christianity Today* 31, no. 18 (December 11, 1987): 17–19.

December 6: Donald J. Shelby, "Meditation: Christmas on Tiptoe," *Christianity Today* 34, no. 18 (December 17, 1990): 32–33.

December 7: Chuck Colson with Catherine Larson, "A Cosmic Culmination: Recalling the Earth-Shaking, Kingdom-Sized Message of Christmas," *Christianity Today* 54, no. 12 (December 2010): 62.

December 8: David Neff, "Misreading the Magnificat," *Christianity Today* 56, no. 11 (December 2012): 61.

December 9: Rodney Clapp, "Let the Pagans Have the Holiday," *Christianity Today* 37, no. 15 (December 13, 1993): 31–32.

December 10: Ruth Bell Graham, "God's Gift on God's Tree," *Christianity Today* 2, no. 5 (December 9, 1957): 14–15.

December 11: Condensed from Bill McKibben, "Christmas Unplugged," *Christianity Today* 40, no. 14 (December 9, 1996): 19–23.

December 12: Addison H. Leitch, "The Prince of Peace," *Christianity Today* 17, no. 6 (December 22, 1972): 4–5.

December 13: Condensed from Billy Graham, "Peace: At Times a Sword and Fire," *Christianity Today* 26, no. 20 (September 5, 1982): 22–25.

December 14: Condensed from Philip D. Yancey, "Hallelujah!: On a Memorable London Night, the Bright and Glistening Theology of *Messiah* Broke through My Jet-Lagged Consciousness," *Christianity Today* 33, no. 18 (December 15, 1989): 30–33.

December 15: Charles Colson with Anne Morse, "The Invasion of God," *Christianity Today* 51, no. 12 (December 2007): 72.

December 16: Condensed from Verne Becker, "Saved by the Bell," *Christianity Today* 34, no. 18 (December 17, 1990): 19–21.

December 17: Condensed from D. Martyn Lloyd-Jones, "His Kingdom Is Forever," *Christianity Today* 2, no. 5 (December 9, 1957): 3–6.

December 18: Walter Wangerin Jr., "Meditation: Painting Christmas," *Christianity Today* 37, no. 15 (December 13, 1993): 28–30.

December 19: Charlotte F. Otten, "Stars on a Silent Night: I Saw the Red Horse at Christmas," *Christianity Today* 5, no. 5 (December 5, 1960): 3–4.

December 20: Walter A. Elwell, "When God Came Down: A Risky Venture," *Christianity Today* 23, no. 27 (December 7, 1979): 16–18.

December 21: Thomas Howard, "On the Festival of Christ's Nativity," *Christianity Today* 18, no. 6 (December 21, 1973): 4–5.

December 22: Thomas C. Oden, "My Dad's Death Brought Christmas 'Home,'" *Christianity Today* 25, no. 21 (December 11, 1981): 20–22.

December 23: Mike Mason, "Yabba-Ka-Doodles!: I'd Begun to Think of Joy as a Hard Taskmistress, and of Christmas as Her Nasty Elder Sister," *Christianity Today* 45, no. 15 (December 3, 2001): 42–44.

December 24: Tim Keller, "The Advent of Humility: Jesus Is the Reason to Stop Concentrating on Ourselves," *Christianity Today* 52, no. 12 (December 2008): 50–53.

December 25: Elisabeth Elliot, "The Wondrous Gift," *Christianity Today* 19, no. 6 (December 20, 1974): 11–13.

December 26: Frank E. Gaebelein, "The Most Beautiful Story Ever Told: Celebration of the Improbable," *Christianity Today* 23, no. 27 (December 7, 1979): 18–20.

December 27: Carolyn Arends, "Our Divine Distortion," *Christianity Today* 53, no. 12 (December 2009): 57.

December 28: Wendy Murray Zoba, "Mary Rejoicing, Rachel Weeping: How Shall We Reconcile the Glorious Birth of the Savior with the Bloody

Deaths of the Boys of Bethlehem?," *Christianity Today* 41, no. 14 (December 8, 1997): 24–26.

December 29: Harold John Ockenga, "Simeon and the Child Jesus," *Christianity Today* 15, no. 6 (December 18, 1970): 4–6.

December 30: James Montgomery Boice, "The Men Who Missed Christmas," *Christianity Today* 17, no. 5 (December 8, 1972): 4–5.

December 31: Philip Yancey, "Ongoing Incarnation," *Christianity Today* 52, no. 1 (January 2008): 60.

January 1: L. Nelson Bell, "Christmas Implications," *Christianity Today* 11, no. 5 (December 9, 1966): 20–21.

January 2: Helmut Thielicke, "Why I Celebrate Christmas," *Christianity Today* 32, no. 18 (December 9, 1988): 21–22.

January 3: Condensed from Timothy George, "The Blessed Evangelical Mary," *Christianity Today* 47, no. 12 (December 2003): 34–39.

January 4: Lee Knapp, "An After-Christmas Gift: A Homeless Man, an Angel, and a Reminder about Our Final Home," *Christianity Today* 47, no. 12 (December 2003): 44–45.

January 5: Jen Pollock Michel, "Not Yet Home for Christmas," *Christianity Today* 59, no. 10 (December 2015): 30.

January 6: Kent R. Hughes, "The Magi's Worship," *Christianity Today* 29, no. 18 (December 13, 1985): 26–28.